BECOMING *the* COMPASS

A Leadership Fable for Emerging Leaders

About the mentors we follow—and the ones we become

RYAN CRITTENDEN, PHD

For permission requests, contact:
XL Coaching and Development
xlcoaching.net

Becoming the Compass: A Leadership Fable
Written by Ryan Crittenden, Ph.D.
First Edition, 2025

ISBN: 979-8-9988771-1-7

For coaching, workshops, or speaking engagements, visit:
xlcoaching.net

To my wonderful, beautiful wife, Bethany—
Thank you for your unwavering love and support. Your belief in me carried this book forward more times than I can count.

To my twin boys, Lucas and Xander—
I'm so glad you are my sons. I am proud of you.

To Dave Mead—
I am incredibly thankful for your friendship. Thank you for being my "Casey."

And to everyone who has ever had a boss like Howard—
You are seen, you are heard, and you are loved. You are not alone.

Table of Contents

PROLOGUE

Every leader has a moment when everything they thought they knew gets flipped upside down. Mine came during a role I loved—in a thriving, entrepreneurial organization. We were getting results. The work mattered. And still, I felt like I was falling apart behind the scenes. Every win came with a whisper: You're still not enough.

I've never felt more alone.

Before that, I wore a uniform. In the Army, I saw every kind of leadership. Some led with rank. Others led with presence. One made people obey. The other made people grow. That contrast stuck with me.

I used to think leadership meant control. Command. Having the answers. Being polished. It worked—until it didn't. Eventually, I met a leader who didn't demand I perform. They made me feel seen. And that changed everything.

That moment taught me: Leadership isn't about pressure—it's about connection. Not authority, but trust. When I stopped trying to impress and started leading with honesty, everything changed. Authenticity didn't weaken me. It made me effective. And free.

This book is rooted in my own journey. The character of Alex? He's me—struggling, second-guessing, recovering. The conversations, the doubts, the quiet breakthroughs? All real. I've been Alex. I try to be Lisa. I pray I'm never Howard. And on my best days, I hope I'm a little like Casey—honest, grounded, human.

Too many new leaders burn out in 18 months. They walk away. Or shut down. I almost did. This story is for anyone who's been there. Anyone healing from toxic leadership. Anyone trying to rebuild from the inside out.

Because when leadership fails, it doesn't just cost results. It costs people—health, families, futures. Leaders shape more than work. They shape lives.

I had to unlearn a lot: that value is earned through performance. That burning bridges means strength. That results matter more than relationships. None of that's true.

Today, I measure success differently. It's when someone says, "You helped me see clearly," or "I see value in my strengths now." That's what lasts.

Forgiveness, vulnerability, second chances—they're all part of leadership, too. Legacy isn't just what you build. It's who you invest in.

I hope this book encourages you. Reminds you what's still right about you. And gives you permission to build something that will outlive you.

One last thing: Every leader needs a mentor, a therapist, and a coach.

If you've never asked for help, start now. Mental health matters. I've seen it—from combat zones to boardrooms to parenting twins. If you're leading anything—especially people—take care of yourself first.

You matter more than you know.

CHAPTER 1

BENEATH THE WEIGHT OF AUTHORITY

The greatest leader is not necessarily the one who does the greatest things. He is the one that gets the people to do the greatest things."

-Ronald Reagan

The meeting room was still, the kind of quiet that didn't come from focus but control. Howard led from the head of the table, posture impeccable, voice smooth and measured. He spoke with the kind of certainty that left little room for deviation, laying out his expectations as if they were already consensus.

Every comment carried a subtle edge, disguised as confidence but designed to shut the door on discussion before it opened. When Jordan cautiously suggested a minor adjustment to the timeline, Howard offered a practiced smile.

"Jordan, I appreciate the initiative," he said, a voice dipped in faux encouragement. "But let's not overcomplicate a process that already works. We stick to the plan—that's how we win."

He didn't raise his voice. He didn't need to. The message was clear: Pushback wasn't welcome. Around the table, team members nodded slowly, but no one leaned forward again. Howard hadn't just led the conversation. He had steered, sealed, and parked it before it ever had a chance to move.

Alex sat midway down the table, observing the interactions with increasing discomfort. The room was heavy with tension, though no one said anything outright. Jordan tapped his pen against the table, his jaw tight. Across from him, Lisa massaged her temples, exhaling as if just sitting here drained her. Mark, who used to crack jokes before meetings, now sat silently, flipping through his notes without looking at them. No one smiled. No one exchanged glances. It felt as though the air had vanished from the room.

From Alex's perspective, it was clear this wasn't a team operating at its best. Howard interrupted constantly and refused to listen, stifling the room and dooming every idea. Alex wondered, *Is this how leadership is supposed to work? Is this the best way to inspire a team?* These questions stuck with him as he watched the meeting unfold, each moment reinforcing the growing disconnect between Howard and his team.

Beyond the conference room, Horizon Valley mirrors the same challenges. Departments barely worked together, employees checked out, and turnover was so bad that the office faced staffing changes every season. Horizon Valley was supposed to be a thriving organization, but it felt stuck, bogged down by inefficiency and sinking morale. Howard's approach to leadership wasn't just affecting this meeting—it was permeating the entire company, creating a culture that felt disjointed and uncertain.

Alex saw the gap between Horizon Valley's potential and current state. He'd joined the organization hoping to make a difference, but meetings like this left him questioning whether that was even possible. The environment felt stagnant, and the lack of trust and openness only exacerbated the situation. It was clear to Alex that something needed to change.

COMMAND WITHOUT CONNECTION

Howard sat at the front of the room, arms crossed and eyes squinted, listening as the team discussed the latest project. His tone was as firm as ever, driving home his expectations without inviting much input.

"We'll follow the plan as outlined," he said, his voice final. "What we need now is execution, not brainstorming."

Jordan shifted in his chair. Despite Howard's apparent preference for sticking to the existing plan, he felt compelled to share an idea he'd been working on—an innovative way to streamline the team's approach by automating part of the workflow.

"Howard, I've been looking into a software solution that could save us significant time on the next phase," he began carefully. "It would reduce the manual steps by about 30%, and I believe it could be implemented without disrupting the current schedule."

Howard didn't even let him get the words out. "We don't need to experiment right now," he said, shaking his head. "Let's stick with what we know works. We can talk about your ideas later."

There was no follow-up and no request for more details. Howard's quick dismissal left Jordan staring at his notes, clearly regretting he'd bothered to speak up. His frustration was palpable, and the rest of the team could sense it as well.

Alex watched the exchange unfold. He saw Jordan's enthusiasm fade as Howard moved on without another word. Alex had seen similar situations. Over time, team members learned that presenting anything beyond their assigned tasks was futile. Howard's need for control left no space for creativity or innovation, and his dismissive reactions sent a clear message: Don't bother.

The results of Howard's leadership style were evident. Jordan, who used to be one of the most outspoken on the team, had gone quiet over the months, only saying what he had to. Others followed suit, keeping their ideas to themselves and sticking to the safe path. The team might have gotten more efficient, but it came at the cost of their energy and motivation. Their morale was visibly low, and Alex couldn't help but notice how their conversations lacked the spark of genuine collaboration.

The effects extended beyond the team. Across Horizon Valley, communication was stagnant, departments operated independently, and innovation had slowed to a crawl. While the organization technically met its goals, its culture felt mechanical, lacking the connection and creativity that had once defined it. This long-term impact on the organization's culture and innovation capacity indicated the need for a sustainable leadership approach.

Howard believed this setup was working just fine. After all, the work was getting done, and there were no significant disruptions. But Alex could see the cracks forming beneath the surface—a team going through the motions, disengaged and uninspired. It left Alex questioning everything he knew about leadership: *Was this the only way to lead, or could there be a better approach?*

CURIOSITY AT THE THRESHOLD

Sitting in the corner of the conference room, Alex couldn't help but notice the growing divide between Howard and the team. Howard's laser-focused approach to control and execution created an invisible wall between him and his employees. While Howard spoke confidently about meeting goals and staying on schedule, Alex observed the team's quiet discomfort. Their subdued responses, lack of eye contact, and minimal engagement told a different story—a team that was disengaged and fearful of speaking up.

After the meeting, Alex grabbed a cup of coffee from the break room. He overheard two employees talking near the doorway.

"Casey actually listens," one of them said. "It's different—you can tell she actually values what we say."

The other nodded. "Yeah. It's weird, right? I'm so used to being dismissed in meetings, but she always asks for input. And not in a fake way, either."

Alex rested his chin on his hand as he thought. He'd never thought much about Casey's meetings before. But now, as he walked toward her department, he slowed down, curiosity nagging at him. What was she doing differently?

Peering through the open door, he watched the interaction unfold.

Casey was standing with a small group, and although they were engaged in a discussion, the energy in the room felt entirely different from Howard's meetings. Casey's open and collaborative leadership style sharply contrasted with Howard's controlling approach, highlighting the impact of different leadership styles on team dynamics.

As Alex leaned against the doorway, he half-expected to see the usual routine—another manager directing orders while the team sat politely, nodding but disengaged. But within seconds, he knew this was different.

Casey wasn't leading like Howard. She wasn't dominating the room or even talking that much. Instead, she leaned forward slightly, her expression open as one of her team members hesitated before speaking.

"What do you think would be the best approach here?" she asked.

Alex expected the team members to react with surprise as if they rarely voiced their opinions. Then, slowly, they outlined an idea. Casey didn't interrupt or correct them. She just nodded, listening, before responding.

Alex leaned in, eyebrows slightly raised. This wasn't just different—it was deliberate. *What was she doing that made people speak so freely?*

Casey smiled and said, "I like where you're going with that—why don't we explore it further and see how it could work?"

Alex lingered near the doorway, watching the interaction unfold. What stood out to him wasn't just Casey's openness and how her team responded to it. No one hesitated to speak up, even when faced with challenges. There was an underlying sense of trust, a belief that their input was valued and respected. Where Howard's meetings felt rigid and tense, Casey's team seemed collaborative and energized.

Alex rubbed the back of his neck as he walked away.

He had expected to see a leader with authority who directed, commanded, and kept things on track. That's what leadership was supposed to be, right?

But Casey's authority came from something else. Not control, but trust. She didn't have to dominate the room because she had already earned their respect.

And as much as Alex hated to admit it. He wasn't sure he could say the same for himself.

Later, he reflected on his observations. Howard's leadership approach was about control—making decisions, dictating the course of action, and ensuring compliance. Casey, on the other hand, emphasized the importance of connection. She built trust by engaging her team in meaningful discussions, encouraging their ideas, and giving them ownership over their work. To Alex, it was clear which approach fostered creativity and engagement and which stifled it.

These observations stayed with Alex, sparking new questions about leadership: *Could he incorporate Casey's relational style into his leadership? How could Horizon Valley, as a whole, move away from the culture of fear that had taken root under Howard's influence?*

Relational Strength

Alex sat alone in the break room, nursing a lukewarm coffee. The day's meetings had left him drained. Watching Howard's controlling leadership style was frustrating and hard to understand. Alex couldn't reconcile how a leader focused on achieving results could create an environment where the team seemed disengaged and uninspired. The problem didn't stop with missed opportunities for creativity. It extended to the feeling that something vital was missing, though he couldn't yet put it into words.

Casey noticed Alex sitting by the back counter, looking drained as he stared into his mug. She hesitated, then crossed the room to join him.

"Long day?" she asked, her voice light but not dismissive.

Alex glanced up, managing a faint smile. "Something like that." He looked back down. "I'm just trying to make sense of what leadership's supposed to look like. Watching Howard? It's hard to tell."

Casey slid into the seat across from him. "What do you think it should look like?"

Alex blinked. "I don't know. I guess not that. But then, I wonder if I'm just being idealistic."

Casey folded her hands, giving him space. "What part of it feels off to you?"

He thought for a moment. "It's like he's always in control, always certain. But it doesn't feel like strength—it feels like no one else gets to think. I keep asking myself if real leadership means shutting people down just to keep things clean."

Casey nodded slowly. "Sounds like what's bothering you isn't just Howard's leadership—it's the gap between what you're seeing and what you believe leadership should be."

Alex sat with that. Then, he said, "Yeah. I think I've been trying to lead without becoming him. But I'm not sure I'm doing it right."

Casey smiled gently. "That's not a bad place to start. The leaders who wrestle with how to lead are often the ones who lead best—because they don't mistake control for strength or silence for unity."

She leaned forward. "So, let me ask you something. What's holding you back from leading the way you want to lead?"

Alex looked away for a second, then back at her. "Maybe. I'm afraid it won't work—that if I lead with trust and empathy, I'll look soft. Or worse—ineffective."

Casey didn't flinch. "Or maybe," she said quietly, "you'll build the kind of team that doesn't flinch around you. Maybe leadership isn't about having all the answers—it's about creating space where the best answers can rise."

Alex didn't respond right away, but something shifted in his posture. Less guarded. A little more grounded.

"Thanks," he said, finally. "I think I needed to hear that."

She stood, touching his shoulder. "You've already started leading differently, Alex. Now, you just have to trust that it's enough."

Alex looked intrigued but skeptical. "That sounds great in theory, but what does it actually look like in practice?"

Casey smiled, this time, with a thoughtful look. "A few years ago, my team was in the middle of a high-stakes project. Tensions were high, and a few team members were butting heads over how to approach one of the deliverables. I could see the frustration building, and I knew if I didn't step in, things would spiral."

She paused, considering her words carefully. "Instead of telling them how to solve it, I brought the group together and created space for everyone to share their concerns. As everyone entered the room, I greeted them, looked them in the eye and told them that I was glad they were there and I was glad to be with them. I listened—really listened—and validated what they were saying, even if I didn't agree with everything. Then, I asked them to find a solution together, offering my support where needed. I didn't dictate the outcome. Instead, I empowered them to work through it as a team."

"And did it work?" Alex asked, genuinely curious.

"It didn't happen right away," Casey admitted. "But after a while, things started to change. They started communicating more openly and even began leaning on each other for support instead of looking to me to mediate. When the project wrapped up, we hit our deadline and came out stronger as a team because of what we worked through. That's the power of relational leadership—it builds trust that lasts beyond the immediate challenge."

Alex sat back, considering her words. It was a striking difference from what he'd seen with Howard, where fear and micromanagement eroded trust and creativity—Casey's way of leading turned problems into chances for the team to grow.

As their conversation paused, Alex finally saw what he'd been missing—a way to lead by connecting with people instead of trying to control them. For the first time in a while, he felt hopeful about what leadership could look like.

PRACTICAL TAKEAWAYS FOR ALEX

Inside the break room, their conversation continued. Casey leaned forward, her tone encouraging but direct. "If you want to start building trust with your team, Alex, you don't need a massive overhaul. Start with small, consistent actions that show you're invested in them as people. Here are three things that have worked for me."

She held up a finger. "First, practice active listening. That means giving people your full attention—no interruptions, no jumping to conclusions. Just hear them out and make sure they know you understand."

Raising a second finger, she added, "Second, celebrate small wins. It doesn't have to be a big production. A simple 'great job on that report' or recognizing someone's effort during a meeting can go a long way in showing that you see and appreciate their contributions."

Finally, Casey held up a third finger. "And third, be consistent. Trust doesn't happen overnight, and it's not about making grand gestures. It's about showing up for your team, day in and day out, in the little ways that matter."

Alex nodded slowly, scribbling notes on the corner of a piece of paper. "It sounds simple, but... I don't know. What if they don't respond right away? What if they don't trust me yet?"

Casey smiled. "That's the thing about trust—it's a process. They might not respond right away, and that's okay. What matters is that you're showing them, through your actions, that you're someone they can rely on. Trust takes time, but every little step moves you closer."

Later, Alex sat at his desk, reflecting on their conversation. He'd always thought of leadership as something you did to drive results, a means to an end—Howard's way of leading strengthened that belief—and leadership as control, leaving no room for collaboration. But Casey had given him a new perspective: leadership as connection, where trust wasn't a byproduct of authority but a deliberate and essential foundation.

Alex thought about the moments in Howard's meetings that had frustrated him the most: the interruptions, the dismissiveness, and the fear he'd seen in his teammates' eyes. Then, he compared it to Casey's team, where collaboration thrived, individuals felt valued, and they were glad to be working together.

Determined to try something new, Alex decided to start small. At their next team meeting, Alex made an intentional effort to listen genuinely. When Jordan shared an idea for improving the team's workflow, Alex paused before responding, ensuring Jordan had finished speaking.

Instead of dismissing the suggestion or jumping in with his thoughts, Alex said, "That's an interesting idea, Jordan. Could you walk us through how you think it might work?"

He noticed a brief flicker of surprise on Jordan's face, followed by a spark of enthusiasm as he explained his idea in more detail. Alex nodded thoughtfully and asked a few follow-up questions, ensuring the discussion remained focused and productive. By the end of the meeting, Alex could feel a slight but noticeable shift in the room. It wasn't a massive shift, but it was progress.

Over the next few days, Alex continued experimenting with Casey's advice. He acknowledged team members' contributions, even for small tasks, and asked about their challenges and successes. Every conversation felt like a step toward something better: building trust and genuine collaboration.

For Alex, these early efforts weren't about overhauling the team overnight. They were about building a foundation, one conversation, one moment at a time. And though it was still early, he could feel the potential of what lay ahead.

FIRST GLIMPSE OF CHANGE

Alex was surprised by how quickly the mood in the office began to shift. It wasn't a dramatic transformation, but his small changes—listening more attentively, acknowledging team members' efforts, and showing consistency in his actions—were starting to show results. During a team meeting, Jordan shared another idea for improving efficiency, and this time, the discussion that followed felt collaborative instead of cautious. Other team members chimed in, building on Jordan's thoughts, and by the end of the meeting, they'd developed a plan that everyone seemed genuinely excited about.

The changes were small, but they mattered. After the meeting, A few team members thanked Alex for facilitating the discussion, and Jordan approached him privately to express his appreciation.

"It feels good to be heard," he said, a smile breaking through his reserved demeanor.

These moments were small victories for Alex, but they carried immense significance. Casey's words helped Alex see that trust develops through small, steady actions. It was slowly taking shape. He was fostering a culture where people felt empowered to share their ideas.

Meanwhile, Howard remained as oblivious as ever to the damage he was causing. During a separate meeting, Alex observed him brushing off a legitimate concern from another team member with his usual dismissive wave.

"I've told you before—just follow the plan," Howard said, his tone leaving no room for discussion.

The team member nodded reluctantly, but frustration was evident in her expression. Howard took the team's silence as a sign that they agreed with him, continuing the meeting as though everything was running smoothly. To Alex, it was a stark reminder of what he wanted to avoid as a leader.

Later, Alex found himself in conversation with Casey again. He shared the small successes he had experienced and the challenges he still faced navigating this new approach. Casey nodded, her expression thoughtful.

"You're on the right path," she said. "Relational leadership is showing up for your team and keeping relationships more important than problems or issues."

Stopping to think, Alex tilted his head, "The opposite would be treating leadership as a transaction with another person."

Casey smiled. "Absolutely. It's about being real, showing who you are, being curious about others and letting your team know you're invested—not just in the results, but in them. That authenticity builds trust like nothing else."

She leaned forward slightly, her tone encouraging. "Here's what I'd challenge you to think about: When your team looks to you, do they see a leader who's just checking boxes, or do they see someone who's genuinely there for them? If you can show up, keeping their relationship with you is more important, everything else starts to fall into place."

Her words stayed with Alex long after their conversation ended. For the first time, he felt a sense of clear direction. Instead of following a list of actions, Alex found a guiding principle for his leadership growth. While the answers weren't all there yet, he began to understand that leadership wasn't about perfection. It was about connection, trust, and, as Casey had emphasized, showing up with authenticity. With this realization, Alex felt ready to take the next step.

As Alex sat back in his chair, reflecting on the conversation with Casey, the weight of what she'd said pressed heavily on his mind. He knew he was on the right path, but the road ahead seemed daunting. The idea of shifting the entire culture of Horizon Valley—from fear-driven compliance to trust-fueled collaboration—felt overwhelming. Would his small steps be enough to make a real difference? Could he convince others, especially Howard, to adopt a leadership style that prioritizes connection over control?

His thoughts were interrupted by the sharp ping of a new email. Without thinking, he clicked it open, his heart sinking as he read the subject line.

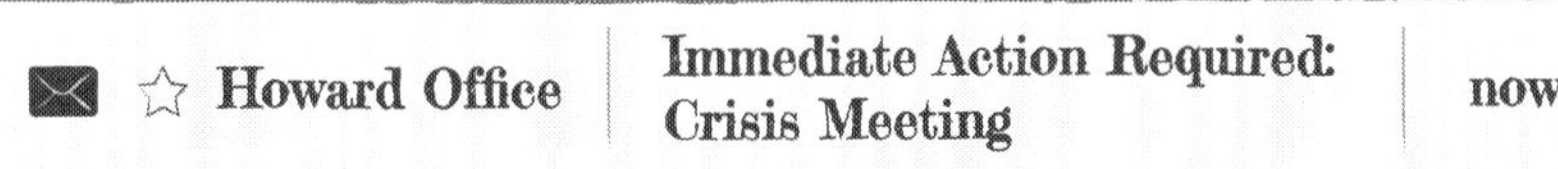

The email was from Howard's office. He clicked it open, scanning the lines as his pulse quickened. A major incident had occurred, necessitating urgent attention.

Alex froze. A gnawing dread replaced the excitement of his recent breakthroughs with the team. He glanced at the clock. Their meeting with Howard was about to begin in 30 minutes.

REFLECT

1. What subtle actions or phrases reveal that Howard's leadership is rooted in fear rather than empowerment? Can you think of a time when you experienced or observed similar leadership?

2. What about Casey's leadership did Alex find so compelling despite its contrast to what he had been taught?

3. What emotions do you think Howard's team members experienced in meetings, and how did this affect their engagement?

4. Casey emphasized trust and relational leadership. How do you currently build trust within your team or workplace?

5. In your current environment, do leaders create space for contributions or dominate dialogue? What does that reveal?

ACTION

1. Identify one behavior from Casey's leadership style that you can implement in your leadership approach today. How will you put it into practice?

2. If you were in Alex's position, what steps would you take to create a more open and engaged team environment?

3. How can you encourage team members to contribute their ideas more freely in meetings?
4. What's one small action you can take this week to recognize or appreciate someone on your team?
5. If you had to mentor someone struggling with a controlling leadership approach, how would you guide them toward a more relational leadership style?

Dear Alex,

Remember that relational leadership is showing up for your team and keeping relationships more important than problems or issues.

From, Casey

CHAPTER 2

RELATIONAL STRENGTH

BUILDING A FOUNDATION

When you lead by fear, you create a culture of compliance. When you lead with trust, you create a culture of commitment."

-Ty Howard

Alex sat at his desk, staring at the untouched notes before him. The latest meeting had ended, but its weight lingered in the air. Across the room, team members moved quietly, some returning to their workstations, others making a beeline for the exit. No one lingered to chat. There were no side conversations—just an underlying sense of exhaustion. He let out a slow breath and leaned back in his chair. *How does this keep happening?*

Howard's meetings were always the same—calm, controlled, and one-sided. His confidence and dominant personality left no room for debate. He had a way of making everything sound logical and convincing. He framed his questions as traps, not invitations for discussion, waiting for someone to stumble so he could reassert his expertise. Howard would twist their words if someone hesitated or misspoke, subtly shifting the conversation to reinforce his position. He didn't raise his voice. His confidence alone made it clear that there was only one way forward—his way.

Alex trained himself to measure his responses, ensuring he never said too much that Howard could twist against him. Howard had been in the industry for decades, after all. The CEO had brought him in to drive results and reshape Horizon Valley into a high-performing machine. On paper, he was doing precisely that. The numbers were good, but Horizon Valley felt like a hollow shell without substance.

Alex had been eager to learn from Howard, drawn to his experience and the way he could subtly command a room. That admiration faded as the months passed. What Alex initially saw as mentorship soon revealed itself as control. Howard wasn't interested in developing a leader. He was shaping a clone. He didn't want Alex to grow. He wanted him to conform.

A movement in the corner of his eye pulled Alex from his thoughts. Howard was going through the office, his usual air of authority intact. As he passed Alex's desk, he muttered, "People just need to work harder," before continuing.

Alex glanced around, taking in the quiet reactions of the team. No one looked up, and no one acknowledged Howard's presence. Across the room, Lisa rubbed her temple. Mark typed aimlessly, deleting and retyping the same line repeatedly. In the break room, Alex overheard two team members whispering to each other.

"I swear, if I have to sit through one more of these meetings, I'm done," one muttered.

"You already applying?" the other asked.

Alex's stomach tightened. They were not only disengaging but also searching for a way out.

The signs had been there, but now the disconnect was fully exposed—Howard had lost them.

The team still showed up and followed instructions, but there was a lack of energy, trust, and genuine connection. People did what was required, but nothing more. No one challenged him, not because they agreed with him but because they had learned it wasn't worth the effort. Howard's leadership style had led to a significant drop in team morale.

Alex exhaled, rubbing a hand over his face. He thought back to Casey and how she led her team—how people gravitated toward her and trusted her enough to be honest and collaborate with her. Leadership doesn't have to be about fear and control. The stark contrast between Howard's authoritarian style and Casey's relational approach was becoming more evident.

But the question remained: How do you build trust when people have already given up on leadership? That question weighed on Alex as he stared at his untouched notes.

Leadership Is a Relationship, Not a Transaction

A few days later, Alex met Casey at the quiet café located on the first floor of Horizon Valley, barely touching his lunch. He needed answers. He had asked to meet because he needed clarity—to understand why her approach to leadership seemed to work when Howard's didn't.

He let out a breath, shaking his head. "Howard focuses on getting things done and burns people out in the process. You focus on people. But doesn't that slow you down?"

Casey smiled, leaning forward slightly. "Actually, it speeds things up. When people trust you, they work harder. They take ownership. They don't need to be forced—they want to do great work."

Alex, thinking intently, slightly shook his head. "But isn't leadership about making sure things get done?"

"Of course," Casey said, nodding. "But here's the thing—trust comes before influence. You can have authority over people, but that doesn't mean they'll follow you. People don't commit to authority. They commit to leaders they trust."

She paused, letting the words settle. "Howard gets compliance, but that's not the same as commitment. You can force people to follow a process, but you can't force them to care." The distinction between compliance and commitment was a crucial insight for Alex, highlighting the true essence of leadership.

Alex mulled that over for a moment. "So, what do you do differently?"

Casey sat back, her expression thoughtful. "I see people as people, not just assets. When you understand the individuals on your team—their strengths, their struggles, their motivations—you don't have to push them to engage. They want to be there. Leadership is no longer a transaction but a relationship."

Alex glanced away, thinking about Howard's meetings. There were no relationships in that room, just directives. People followed instructions but never went beyond the bare minimum. There was no connection.

Seeing his expression, Casey continued, "Let me give you an example. A few years ago, I took over a team that was completely disengaged. They weren't necessarily bad at their jobs, but you could tell they were just going through the motions. Meetings were lifeless, collaboration was nonexistent, and morale was low."

Alex nodded. "Sounds familiar."

Casey smirked. "I could have come in and started demanding results, but that would've been a mistake. Instead, I spent the first few weeks meeting with each team member one-on-

one—no agenda, no immediate changes—just listening and asking questions. I asked about their experiences, their frustrations, and what motivated them. At first, they were skeptical, but over time, something shifted. They started to trust that I actually cared, and engagement naturally followed when that trust was built. I didn't have to force it."

"So, just by talking to them, you got them to work harder?" Alex asked.

"Not just talking—understanding," Casey corrected. "When people feel heard and understood, they invest in their work differently. They take responsibility for their success, not because they have to, but because they want to. That's the difference between leadership through control and leadership through connection."

Alex sat back in his chair, running a hand through his hair. Leadership as connection. A simple idea, but it didn't exist in Howard's world.

And that's precisely why everything at Horizon Valley felt broken.

Casey reached into her bag and pulled out a small, cream-colored envelope. She slid it across the table to Alex.

"What's this?" he asked, eyeing it curiously.

"Just something that reminded me of you," she said. "Don't open it now. Later—when it feels right."

He turned the envelope over in his hand. It was light but not empty. "Is this a symbolic thing?"

She smiled, already standing. "Let's call it a reminder. Every leader needs one now and then."

With that, she patted the table gently and walked away—no grand exit, just presence. But something about the envelope lingered, heavy in its meaning.

Alex tucked it into his notebook without opening it. *Not yet.*

Small Shifts, Big Impact

Alex settled back into his office desk, still thinking about his conversation with Casey. He knew relational leadership required small, consistent actions rather than grand gestures or overnight changes. It was about the small moments, the way a leader showed up day after day.

Alex noticed Lisa's posture—tense, shoulders hunched, her screen untouched. Something was off. Lisa had been with Horizon Valley for a few years and had earned a reputation as one of the most capable members of the team. She was sharp, detail-oriented, and efficient—someone who, under different circumstances, could probably be a future leader herself. Lately, however, Alex has noticed a change.

She had stopped offering ideas in meetings. She no longer lingered to chat with colleagues. The enthusiasm she had when he first started at Horizon Valley had faded into something else—detachment. It wasn't that her work had suffered. She still managed to get things done. But there was a difference between doing the job and being invested in it, and Lisa had checked out.

Alex hesitated. His instinct, ingrained from years of working under Howard, was to let her figure it out on her own. If she had a problem, she'd solve it or deal with the consequences. That was the way things worked here.

But then, he heard Casey's words: *"Start by listening and asking."*

Instead of walking past, he stopped by Lisa's desk. "Hey," he said casually. "I noticed something different about you. How are you doing today?"

Lisa froze mid-typing as if she wasn't sure if she should answer. "Honestly? I'm unsure if I'm doing this right, but I was afraid to ask."

Alex frowned slightly. "What makes you afraid to ask?"

Lisa gave a slight, almost embarrassed shrug. "Because around here, you look weak if you ask for help."

That answer hit harder than Alex expected. It wasn't about the project. It was about the culture. People weren't just hesitant to collaborate—they were afraid to admit they didn't have all the answers.

Instead of giving her a quick fix or reminding her to "just get it done," Alex took a different approach. "I don't think asking for help is weak," he said. "If anything, it means you care about what you are doing."

Lisa studied him for a moment as if waiting for the catch. When none came, her shoulders relaxed slightly. "I guess I never thought of it that way."

It was a slight shift, but Alex saw it happen in real time—Lisa's guard lowered even a little. She wasn't used to being heard.

Across the room, Jordan watched from his desk, arms crossed, his face unreadable. He hadn't spoken much in weeks, but when he did, it was usually to question—not contribute. With a quiet scoff, he muttered, "Man, you're wasting your time. You think caring is gonna get you a promotion?"

Alex turned to face him and asked, "What if people do better work when they don't feel like they're constantly being tested?"

Jordan scoffed. "You really think listening and playing nice is gonna change anything? Howard gets results. That's what matters."

Alex swallowed the retort rising in his throat. He could feel eyes on him, waiting to see how he'd respond. If he backed down now, he'd prove Jordan right.

"What if results come from trust, not fear?" Alex countered. "You ever think about how much better we'd work if we didn't have to second-guess every word in meetings?"

Jordan folded his arms. "Yeah, well. Good luck with that." But for the first time, Alex caught a flicker of doubt in his expression.

Alex didn't argue. He couldn't. Jordan had a point—this was Howard's world, and Howard's way ruled. People knew how to survive here—stay quiet, do your job, don't get noticed for anything that could make Howard look bad.

A few others glanced over, clearly aware of the exchange but keeping their distance. Alex could sense their hesitation. He wasn't the first person to try something different. Others had tried to lead similarly to the way Casey leads. However,

Howard had enforced his way for so long that most people stopped believing leadership could be different.

And for a moment, doubt crept in.

What if Jordan's right? What if caring made him seem weak? He'd seen it happen before—managers who tried to connect and lead with relationships, only to be steamrolled by company culture. Was he setting himself up for the same?

But then, he remembered Lisa's reaction. She relaxed, if only slightly, as soon as she realized no one was judging her.

Howard's leadership kept people in a state of survival, but Lisa's reaction told Alex something important: People needed someone to listen and understand.

And that was enough to keep going.

CHAPTER 2

DEEPENING TRUST THROUGH CONSISTENCY

A week later, Alex met with Casey before work. At the café table, he sat with his arms crossed, and frustration was evident as he tried to get his words together. Casey stirred her coffee, giving him time and space to say what was on his mind.

"I tried, but people aren't buying it," Alex finally admitted. "I asked Lisa how she was doing, I made a real effort to listen, but it still feels like everyone is waiting for me to fail. Like they don't trust that I actually mean it."

Casey didn't look surprised. "How long has Howard been leading with fear?"

Alex sighed. "Years."

"And how long have you been leading differently?"

He glanced down at his watch, then let out a short laugh. "A few hours."

Casey didn't look surprised. She just gave a knowing smile. "Now you're getting it."

She set her coffee down and met his eyes. "People don't trust change overnight, Alex. And certainly not in a few hours. If all they've ever known is leadership by control, they won't suddenly believe a different approach will last. It's not that they don't want things to improve or even be different. It's that they've seen too many people give up and go back to what's easy."

Alex nodded slowly, his frustration shifting into something else. Howard's leadership wasn't the only problem. The real challenge? Undoing years of fear.

Casey continued, "You don't have to prove yourself with some grand gesture. Small, consistent actions build credibility. Don't try to convince them in one conversation. It's about showing up, day after day, and being the leader you say you want to be."

He took a deep breath. "So, what do I do in the meantime?"

"Stay the course," Casey said. "Even when it feels like no one notices. Even when it feels like nothing's changing. Because the second you stop, you'll prove them right—that leaders don't care, they just pretend to until it gets hard. Remember to keep relationships bigger than problems."

Alex let her words sink in. It was the opposite of Howard's style, where leadership was about demanding results and moving on. But Casey was right. Trust wasn't something you declared. It was something you earned.

Later that day, Alex sat in on another meeting, watching Howard lead the discussion. It was the usual routine: Howard talking, the team listening, with little to no real engagement. But today, something different happened.

Mark, one of the more experienced team members, had missed a deadline. He wasn't known for that—quite the opposite. Over the years, Mark had become one of the steadiest hands at Horizon Valley. Quiet, reliable, and unfailingly thorough. If he'd missed something, it wasn't out of carelessness.

But Howard didn't pull him aside. He addressed the issue in front of the entire project team.

Howard tapped the report in his hand, then looked up slowly. "You know, I've built a career on consistency," he said, his tone even but cool. "I've always believed that a true professional knows how to stay ahead of the curve—no matter what's going on."

He paused, letting the silence linger before continuing. "Now, I'm not here to point fingers. But when timelines slip, it's usually a sign that someone's gotten a little too comfortable."

Mark didn't flinch, but the set of his jaw tightened.

Howard gave a small, clipped smile. "I know you've been around a long time, Mark. Maybe that's part of the problem. Familiarity can make people forget what excellence looks like."

Howard didn't shout the words, but they cut just the same. Mark gave a single nod, his eyes fixed on the table, saying nothing.

Howard moved on as if it were just another bullet point. But everyone in the room felt the shift, quiet and sharp. The moment reminded everyone who held the power—and how easily he could use it to diminish rather than develop.

No one spoke. No one defended Mark. The entire room held still, bracing for Howard to move on.

Alex felt the weight of the moment and wondered if he could have done something. Howard thought he was leading and reinforcing accountability, but he ensured that no one would ever admit to struggling again.

As the meeting ended and people gathered their things, Alex saw Mark still seated and staring at his notes. He was disengaged and checked out.

Howard might get people to comply, but obedience and trust aren't the same.

Alex knew then that Casey was right. Leadership centered on control will crumble easily. It was about trust, and trust grows with time.

ALEX'S COMMITMENT TO GROWTH

The office was mainly empty, and Alex was shutting down his computer when he heard a quiet voice behind him.

"Hey..."

He turned to see Lisa standing near his desk, shifting her weight slightly, unsure whether to say what was on her mind.

"Just wanted to say thanks for talking with me last week," she said, her voice softer than usual. "It actually helped."

Alex blinked, caught off guard. "Really?"

Lisa gave a subtle nod. "Yeah. It's the first time someone asked how I was doing before talking about my work."

Her words landed heavier than Alex expected. He had barely done anything—just asked a simple question, listened, and let her know she wasn't alone. But to her, it mattered. That realization settled in his chest as Lisa walked away. It was such a small moment, yet it confirmed what Casey had told him.

Leadership wasn't about grand gestures or forcing people to follow orders. It was about connection, about building trust in the smallest of interactions. He didn't need to demand respect like Howard—he just had to earn it, one person at a time.

That evening, Alex replayed the moment in his mind and started to see the bigger picture: Howard had led Horizon Valley through control, keeping people compliant but disengaged. And while that approach had kept things moving on the surface, it had cost the company something far more significant.

The silence in meetings, the lack of collaboration, and the way people like Lisa hesitated to ask for help stemmed from a lack of trust. Rebuilding that trust would take time, but it was possible.

The next day, Alex caught up with Casey in the hallway, his pace quick, his voice energized. "I think I get it now," he said. "Building trust is slow, but it's the foundation. If people don't trust you, nothing else really works."

Casey smiled, but didn't nod. Instead, she asked, "Okay—but once they trust you, who are they trusting you to be?"

Alex blinked, caught off guard. "What do you mean?"

She paused, lightly tapping the folder in his hand. "You've been clear about what kind of leader you don't want to be. But have you figured out what kind of leader you want to be?"

Alex didn't answer right away. The question sat with him longer than expected. Alex focused so much on avoiding Howard's example that he never stopped to define his own. Casey gave a slight nod and kept walking. Alex stood in place, still holding the question—and beginning to realize it might be the most important one yet.

All these new concepts about leadership swirled around inside his head. It was about connection, trust, and the smallest moments. People wouldn't change their views immediately, and skepticism was usual. He thought about Lisa's hesitation, Jordan's doubt, and the wary looks of others—it was all part of the process. But if one conversation could make a difference, maybe more of them could, too.

As Alex slowly gained confidence, Casey continued to mentor with wisdom, reinforcing that relational leadership required patience. Jordan, however, resisted change, clinging to the belief that leadership meant projecting strength and maintaining control. And Howard? He doubled down on control, determined to keep running things his way.

But something had shifted. Horizon Valley wasn't the same as it had been before. Howard's hold on the team wasn't as strong as it used to be. Alex could see the cracks forming.

Things were just getting started.

REFLECT

1. How did Howard's leadership style continue to reinforce fear and disengagement among his team? Have you ever worked in an environment where people hesitated to share ideas, ask for help, or feared public humiliation?

2. Lisa hesitated to ask for help because she feared looking weak. What does this say about the culture of a workplace? How does fear-based leadership impact growth and innovation?

3. Think about when you had to build trust with a team or colleague. What actions helped strengthen that trust? How did Casey's perspective on leadership challenge Alex's assumptions, and what did that reveal about his growth?

4. What small moments in leadership have made the most significant impact in your own experiences, and how do they compare to the shifts Alex was making?

ACTION

1. Alex began using relational leadership by asking Lisa how she was doing. What steps can you take today to build trust with your team or colleagues, even in a challenging work environment?

2. Casey told Alex that small, consistent actions build credibility. What is one small leadership habit you can commit to practicing consistently over the next month?

3. If you notice someone on your team struggling, how can you approach them in a way that fosters support rather than fear?

4. Consider Howard's leadership style. How can you challenge the culture of "fear of failure" or "fear of

asking for help" within your team? What changes in communication or support structures would help?

5. Casey told Alex, "Now, you have to figure out what kind of leader you want to be." Take a moment to reflect—what kind of leader do you want to be, and what actions can you take to embody that?

To Alex,

When people trust you, they work harder. They take ownership. They don't need to be forced–they want to do great work.

Always, Casey

CHAPTER 3

AUTHENTIC PRESENCE

LEADING WITHOUT MASKS

It's hard to lead a cavalry charge if you think you look funny on a horse."

-Adlai E. Stevenson

Alex sat at the conference table, hands clasped, trying to keep up as the conversation sped past him. Every time he thought of speaking, the moment slipped away, leaving him tense and unsure. Howard replaced these moments with another sharp comment or quick decision.

"Strong leaders don't hesitate," Howard liked to say.

As Alex watched the dynamic play out, he caught Jordan's eye from across the table. Jordan leaned back in his chair, expression unreadable, but his words from their last conversation echoed in Alex's mind: "Being nice won't get you ahead."

Alex shifted in his seat, his mind a battleground of conflicting thoughts. *Was Jordan right? Did leadership mean shutting off the part of him that listened, cared, and built trust? Do I need to be more like Howard—blunt, unwavering, and unemotional—to prove myself?*

His stomach tightened at the thought.

Howard continued speaking, moving through the agenda with practiced authority. He barely glanced at the people around him, confident that his way was right. When someone hesitated to respond, Howard filled the silence, pressing forward as if their input didn't matter. At one point, he nodded toward Jordan. "Strong leaders know how to take control. They don't waste time second-guessing." His eyes flicked toward Alex briefly, but the message was clear.

Alex clenched his jaw. He'd spent weeks leading with trust instead of control, but now, doubt crept in. As the meeting dragged on, that doubt tightened. Maybe he'd been wrong. Maybe his style wasn't his strength—it was the reason he felt stuck. Howard's way got results. And for the first time, Alex wasn't sure which path to trust.

THE STRUGGLE TO LEAD AUTHENTICALLY

Alex stood at the front of the small meeting room, his hands resting on the table. Although he had led meetings before, today felt different. Today, he was testing a new approach that resembled Howard's.

He scanned his team's faces, noting how they settled into their seats. Lisa sat near the middle, her expression neutral but alert. Mark, a steady presence in the group, leaned back slightly in his chair. Others glanced at their notes, waiting for him to begin.

Alex stood straight. If he wanted people to take him seriously, he needed to lead like someone in control.

"We need to tighten things up," he started, keeping his voice steady and firm. "I've looked at the latest timelines, and we can't afford to keep going at this pace. We have to move faster."

A few people exchanged glances. Lisa's head tilted as if weighing his words.

"We're not here to overthink or second-guess," he continued. "Just focus on getting things done."

His words came out sharper than intended, but he pushed forward. He kept his instructions short and direct. When someone hesitated before responding, he filled the silence before they could. When a question veered off track, he cut it short and moved on.

It was how Howard ran his meetings—efficient, no wasted time. But instead of feeling like he was leading, Alex felt like he was performing.

Lisa sat up straighter at first, nodding as Alex spoke. But as his tone sharpened, her expression flickered—just for a second. She glanced at her notes, flipping a page she hadn't read. She shifted in her chair, crossing her arms loosely when he cut off a question mid-sentence. She had been one of the first to engage when he truly listened. Now, hesitation clouded her face. Still, he stuck with it.

As Alex pushed the team forward with sharp directives, Mark, who usually asked the most questions, opened his mouth—then closed it again. He glanced at Lisa as if waiting for her to speak up instead. Across the table, a junior team member tapped their pen against the notepad, their leg bouncing slightly under it.

When someone was concerned, Alex said, "Let's not drag this out," and pressed forward. The silence that followed wasn't the usual pause before someone spoke. It lingered, thick and unmoving. Lisa glanced toward Mark, who tapped his fingers against the table, his gaze fixed on a spot just past Alex's shoulder. No one rushed to fill the gap. When Alex finally moved on, the energy in the room had already shifted.

As the meeting came to a close, Lisa gathered her notes more slowly than usual. Pausing briefly, she watched Alex as if weighing whether to speak. With a short, not-so-confident nod, Lisa turned and left.

Alex sat down, rubbing the back of his neck. He had expected to feel more in control, but felt a profound disconnection from the team and himself. *Howard's approach got results, but was this really what leadership was supposed to feel like?*

THE MATURITY QUESTION

Alex needed air. The meeting was over, but the tension clung to him, following him out the door. The air was crisp, and he let himself breathe for a moment. He had done what Howard would have—taken control and pushed for results—but instead of feeling like a leader, he felt like he was playing a role that didn't fit.

Casey approached from across the courtyard, her pace unhurried. At first, she said nothing. She fell into step with him as they walked. After a few moments, she broke the silence, offering a different perspective on leadership.

"Hey, how'd that sales meeting go?" she asked, seeming to know the answer.

Alex gave her a side-eye.

"I saw you in the meeting," she said. "That wasn't you."

Alex exhaled, his hands shoved in his pockets. "I was just trying to be more assertive."

Casey didn't hesitate. "You're not leading—you're rehearsing. And people can tell."

Alex didn't answer immediately, keeping his eyes forward as the pavement blurred beneath him. The urge to push back sat heavy in his chest—to say he was doing what worked. But deep down, the truth was undeniable. Casey was right.

Casey raised an eyebrow. "Have you ever had a friend who acted one way with you and a different way in front of a crowd?"

Alex nodded. "Yeah, it's weird."

She smirked. "Exactly. Leadership is the same way. People don't buy the act—they buy the real deal.

"Do you think people follow leaders because they talk the loudest or because they trust them the most?" Casey asked.

They walked in silence for a moment before Casey said, "People don't follow a performance, Alex. They follow leaders who know who they are—leaders who don't need to prove it."

Alex nodded. "Howard's confident."

Casey paused, then tilted her head. "Confident, or just used to having power?"

Alex's brow furrowed. He hadn't considered that distinction. "I'm not sure."

Casey gave a slight nod. "Might be worth figuring out."

Alex remembered the previous meetings and how Howard had dominated the room. There was no doubt that Howard believed in himself, but was that the same thing as creating trust?

They reached a bench near the courtyard's edge, and Casey motioned for him to sit. She tapped her fingers against her knee, thinking.

She smiled. "I once believed I had to conform to a specific mold to earn respect. I'd watch other leaders—those who commanded attention and spoke with authority—and figure, "That's how they do it." So, I adjusted. I spoke differently and acted differently. If I played the part, people would respect me more."

Alex waited, sensing there was more.

"The problem?" she continued. "It didn't work. Instead of gaining credibility, I started losing it. People could tell something was off. I wasn't fooling anyone. I stopped trying to be someone else. I led from my strengths—honesty, connection, trust. And you know what happened? People followed me, not because I was trying to be powerful, but because they knew who they were getting every time."

Casey exhaled, watching a few leaves scatter in the wind. "You know, leadership isn't about looking the part," she said. "It's about showing up as yourself—consistently. No masks, no performance. Just you."

She paused, then added, "But the only way to always be yourself in leadership is to grow in maturity. Because without maturity, it's too easy to lead from fear, ego, or insecurity."

Alex leaned back, the words catching him off guard.

"Mature leaders," Casey continued, "know who they are. They're emotionally grounded. They invest in their people's strengths and take care of those they lead. Immature leaders do the opposite—they take advantage of people, exploit their weaknesses, and call it strategy."

She looked at him directly. "So, what kind of leader do you want to be?"

Alex didn't answer right away. He realized the question wasn't just about leadership style. It was about growth—his own.

Learning from Failure

Casey leaned forward. "This reminds me of a time I really messed up."

Alex blinked—Casey didn't seem like someone who made big mistakes.

She smirked. "Oh, it was bad. We were launching a major system change. I had a perfect plan—until Bobby skipped a step. He thought he was helping. Instead, the system crashed, and everything shut down."

Alex winced. "What did you do?"

"I could've made an example of him—what Howard would've done. But Bobby already knew he screwed up. He didn't need punishment—he needed perspective." She paused. "So, I took the hit publicly. Bobby needed to know he wasn't a problem, just that we had a problem to solve. So, I pulled him aside and asked, 'How can we fix this?'"

Alex frowned. "And that worked?"

"A year later, Bobby caught a similar issue before it became a problem. He took initiative, owned it, and brought me a solution."

She let that sink in. "If I'd crushed him to prove a point, he would've shut down. Instead, he grew."

Alex folded his arms. "Try that here, you'll get steam-rolled."

Casey shrugged. "Maybe that's the real problem."

He thought of Howard—of how fear shaped every meeting. Mistakes were punished, not learned from. No wonder the team avoided risk.

"So, what—just let things slide?" Alex asked.

"Not at all. Accountability matters. But fear isn't leadership, and people aren't problems. You build culture through example, not control."

Alex sat quietly. For the first time, he saw it: They weren't disengaged because they didn't care. They were disengaged because they didn't feel safe to try.

THE SHIFT: ALEX REDEFINES LEADERSHIP FOR HIMSELF

The office hum faded into the background as Alex tried to regain focus on his work. Casey's words echoed, forcing him to confront a truth he had avoided—this version of leadership didn't fit. The moment he stepped into Howard's shoes, everything felt wrong. He had seen it in his team's faces, in Lisa's hesitation, and in the strained silence that followed his last meeting.

For weeks, he had been trying to prove that he was strong enough to lead, as if leadership was about projecting authority instead of earning trust. Howard made it clear what kind of leader got results. Jordan reinforced the idea that being "nice" would hold him back. So, he started molding himself into what he thought leadership was supposed to look like—forceful, controlled, and unshaken.

But that wasn't who he was.

He leaned back in his chair, rubbing his temples as he thought about the qualities that had made people trust him in the past. He was at his best when listening, helping people see the bigger picture, and building relationships instead of just enforcing rules. Those weren't weaknesses. They were the things that made him valuable as a leader.

For the first time, everything fell into place. Leadership wasn't about playing a role but about showing up fully. There was no need to mimic Howard's approach or follow Jordan's advice. His strength had never come from being the loudest in the room but from fostering an environment where people wanted to contribute. And maybe that was the real difference.

People followed Howard because they had to. Alex wanted them to follow because they wanted to.

Alex picked up his pen and flipped to a clean page in his notebook. He wrote: "What does leadership look like if I do it my way?"

The answer wasn't immediate, but he wasn't questioning everything for the first time in weeks.

Chapter 3

Alex Tries Again—This Time as Himself

Alex stood at the head of the conference table with a smile, watching as his team trickled into the room. The last time they had gathered like this, he had tried to take control, to lead with authority rather than authenticity. It hadn't gone well. He had felt it, and his team had, too. This time, he was doing things differently.

Once everyone had settled, he took a breath and started with the truth. "I think I got it wrong last time," he said. "I tried leading in a way that didn't feel like me, and I could tell it didn't sit well with you either. That's on me."

He let the words settle. His team looked at him, surprised, but no one interrupted.

"I want to make sure we're working together, not just running through tasks," he continued. "So, let's take a step back. What's working? What's not? What are we doing that we need to stop doing?"

Silence stretched for a beat, and Alex wondered if they were hesitating, waiting for the usual directive. Then, Lisa shifted in her chair and spoke up. "I appreciate you saying that, Alex. Last time, it felt like no one was listening. But this—this feels different."

Alex smiled and nodded, relieved she had picked up on the shift.

Mark leaned forward. "Honestly, I think we're all just used to being told what to do and moving forward without much discussion. But that's not necessarily the best way to work."

The experience confirmed for Alex that Howard had built a culture where people complied without engaging.

"So, let's change that," Alex said. "If something isn't working, I want to know. We can't fix problems we don't talk about."

The conversation started slowly, but honest discussions unfolded as the team warmed up to the topic. People spoke more freely, offering insights instead of waiting for instructions. Alex found himself leaning in, listening, asking questions instead of directing, and engaging instead of correcting. The room was full of people working together for the first time in weeks, not just completing tasks.

HOWARD REACTS

Alex felt a rare lightness after the meeting—until he spotted Howard by the break room, arms crossed, waiting. Their eyes met, and Howard gave a short nod before speaking. "I heard about your meeting today," he said, his tone unreadable.

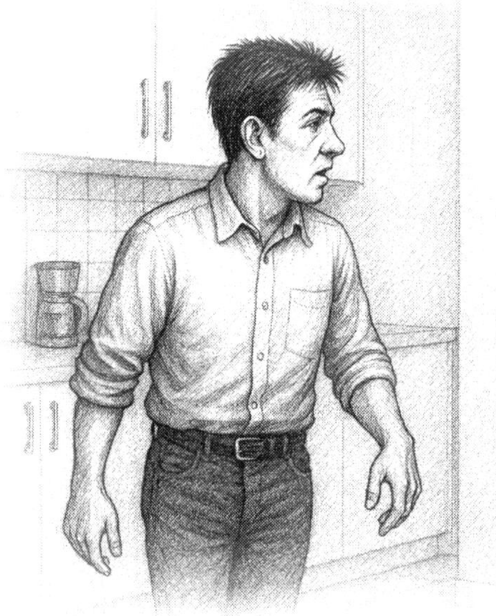

Alex met his gaze evenly. "Great. What did you hear?"

Howard crossed his arms and let out a dry chuckle, shaking his head, his expression sharp. "You think this type of teamwork will hold up when things get tough?" He leaned in slightly, lowering his voice. "They'll respect you when you make the hard calls, not when you hold their hands."

There was a time when those words would have planted doubt in Alex's mind. He would have repeatedly replayed them a week ago, questioning if he was doing the right thing. But not this time.

Howard's team did as expected. No risks. No questions. Alex had already seen the difference between people feeling heard and when they felt invested in the work.

Alex felt the old hesitation rising, that instinct to prove himself to Howard, to seek approval. But then, he thought of his team and Lisa's trust, which was beginning to rebuild. He met Howard's gaze. "I'm not here to prove myself to you. I'm here to lead them."

Howard's lips pressed into a thin line. He studied Alex briefly, his usual quick response held back, just for a beat. It wasn't long, but it was enough for Alex to recognize it. Howard was assessing and measuring him—and maybe, for the first time, realizing Alex wasn't backing down.

Alex watched him leave, a novel resolve stirring within. Dominance or rigid control no longer defined leadership—at last, a more authentic style emerged.

Leadership Without Masks

The office had settled into its usual rhythm—keyboards clicking, conversations humming, phones ringing in the background. Alex sat at his desk, his computer and notes from the meeting still open before him, though he hadn't touched them in the last 10 minutes. His mind was elsewhere, replaying the conversations from earlier.

He felt like he was heading in the right direction. He didn't need to prove anything and hadn't tried to sound tougher or more in control than he was. Somehow, that worked better than anything else he had tried. His team responded better, not out of obligation, but because they felt heard.

The sound of approaching footsteps pulled him from his thoughts. He glanced up to see Lisa standing near his desk, arms crossed, with a thoughtful expression.

"I almost lost trust in you after last time," she said without preamble. "But today? I think you're onto something."

Alex blinked, taken aback by her honesty. He could tell she wasn't just saying it to be nice—Lisa wasn't the type to offer empty praise.

"Thanks," he said, setting his pen down. "I wasn't sure how it would go."

Lisa nodded. "Neither were we." Her voice had no edge, just a simple statement of fact. "It's just last time, it felt like you were trying too hard to be something you're not. But today, it felt like you meant it."

Alex let that sink in. It wasn't just about how he felt leading, but about how his team experienced his leadership. And they could tell the difference.

Lisa offered a brief nod before departing. As Alex watched her leave, a profound feeling welled within him. For too long, he had struggled to conform to a rigid ideal of leadership that never truly fit. In reality, that very ideal had become his obstacle. Rather than proving his worth, he realized that embodying leadership was enough.

Later that afternoon, Alex noticed Casey standing by the coffee machine, absentmindedly stirring a mug. When Alex walked past the break room, Casey glanced up.

"You survived," she said with a smirk.

Alex chuckled. "I think I might have done more than that."

Casey grinned. "Feels better, doesn't it?"

"It really does," he admitted. "I was so caught up in what I thought leadership was supposed to be that I never stopped to think about what actually works for me."

She tilted her head, studying him for a beat before speaking. "Sometimes, it's not just about knowing who you are when things are easy. The real test comes when things get difficult and true hardship happens."

Alex raised an eyebrow. "That sounds ominous."

"Not ominous. Just reality." Casey set her mug down and crossed her arms. "Leadership isn't just about when things are easy. It's about keeping relationships more important than problems and having the ability to come back to yourself when everything's falling apart."

The shift in conversation made Alex pause. He had spent so much time figuring out how to lead authentically, but he hadn't considered what would happen when things didn't go according to plan.

Casey took a step toward the door. "You've found your footing, Alex. But can you stand your ground when the storm hits?" She didn't wait for an answer. She just gave him a knowing look before walking away.

Alex let out a breath. He'd taken the first step—but Casey was right. Confidence alone wouldn't be enough.

He turned back to his desk, finally picking up his pen—not to jot down notes or check another box, but to reflect. He opened a fresh page in his notebook and wrote a single question at the top: "What kind of mindset sustains authentic leadership?"

Leadership wasn't just about what you did in the moment. It was about how you thought, how you saw people, and how you showed up—again and again.

REFLECT

1. How did Alex's attempt to mimic Howard's leadership style backfire? Have you ever tried to act a particular way to fit an expected leadership mold? How did it affect your confidence and the way others responded to you?

2. Have you ever worked with someone who led differently depending on their audience? How did that impact trust?

3. Lisa initially lost trust in Alex after his failed attempt at leading the meeting. What does this reveal about how fragile trust can be? Have you ever experienced a leader earning back trust after a misstep? What did they do differently?

4. Reflect on Howard's conversation with Alex. Why do some leaders associate toughness with credibility? How does that mindset affect team morale and long-term engagement?

5. Alex's breakthrough moment came when he acknowledged and leveraged his natural leadership strengths. Think about a time when you leaned into your strengths instead of trying to fit someone else's leadership mold. How did it change the way you led or influenced others?

Action

1. Alex shifted his leadership style by admitting his mistake and listening to his team. Identify one way you can make your leadership more authentic this week. What steps can you take today to show vulnerability and build stronger trust with your team?

2. Howard's leadership style created a culture of compliance, while Alex is working toward building trust and

engagement. What specific actions can you take in your leadership to create an environment where people feel safe to contribute?

3. Casey handled Bobby's mistake by treating him as a person, not a problem. How can you support a team member who has made a mistake while still holding them accountable for learning and growth?
4. Jordan dismissed Alex's leadership shift as weak. How do you stay committed to leading authentically, even when faced with skepticism or resistance?
5. How would you sum up your leadership philosophy in one sentence, and how do you plan to practice it?

My friend Alex,

People don't buy the act–they buy the real deal.

From, Casey

CHAPTER 4

PURPOSEFUL RESILIENCE

STAYING GROUNDED

Pressure doesn't build leaders–perspective does."

-John Maxwell

Alex stood at the edge of the mezzanine, hands gripping the metal railing as he surveyed the bullpen below. Rows of cubicles and glass-walled offices stretched out beneath him, a maze of flickering computer screens and furrowed brows. The usual hum of conversation faded, giving way to the quiet tension of a team grappling with an impossible task. The CEO of Horizon Valley unveiled new objectives, accompanied by higher revenue and profit targets. The deadline was tight. They were behind.

A few weeks ago, things were moving smoothly. The team had a plan, roles were clear, and momentum was building. Then came the setbacks—miscommunication between departments, missed details, and last-minute adjustments. Each issue chipped away at progress, leaving them scrambling to catch up.

Now, pressure was at its peak. However, the pressure did not seem to touch Howard. He was calm and collected. He was able to communicate with the CEO and executive team with ease and confidence. However, Alex noticed a difference in how he interacted with the team he led.

Howard paced the room and called his newly added department heads, Alex, Lisa, Jordan, and Mark, into the conference room. "We cannot afford to miss the revenue and profit goals," he stated, squinting his eyes at the team. "This isn't complicated. Let's get this nailed down. If anyone on your team has an issue, put them on a performance plan or show them the door."

The room wasn't silent out of focus—it was silent out of caution.

Alex's instincts kicked in—tighten control, push harder, force results. That used to work. But Casey's voice echoed in his mind: Authentic leadership isn't about power but connecting.

How do I keep people engaged when everything's going wrong? The question hit hard. Alex felt an old instinct rise—act fast, take control. But deeper down, he knew better. Fear doesn't lead. It only reacts. And that wasn't the kind of leader he wanted to be anymore.

His mind returned to Casey's words: *"Leadership is about keeping your relationships with your people more important than problems."*

PURPOSEFUL RESILIENCE

Alex stepped out of the building, the cold air a welcome contrast to the heat rising in his chest. He had an overwhelmed team, a deadline that wouldn't move, and a choice to lean into the panic or find a better way.

He overlooked Casey until she spoke. "Hey, are you okay?" Alex just stared, unable to find the words to say. "Let's take a walk." Casey's voice was calm and steady. The kind of steady he wished he had.

Alex didn't argue. He fell into step beside her, waiting for her to say something. But she didn't. Instead, they walked silently through the side path around the building. The quiet stretched, and Alex felt like he could breathe for the first time all day.

After a few moments, he finally spoke. "I thought that leadership wasn't about avoiding problems but how you respond to them. But how do you stay calm when everything is falling apart?"

Casey let out a slow breath, hands deep in her coat pockets. "If you love coming to work, there is joy in being with your people and delight in accomplishment."

Alex huffed, shaking his head. "Yeah, I'm failing this test so far."

"How are you feeling, Alex?"

Alex looked down and collected his thoughts. He took a deep breath and plainly said, "I am stressed and have feelings of anxiety building up when I am here. It doesn't seem to go away."

Casey stopped walking and turned to face him. "I can see that you're stressed and anxious. That's completely understandable. You're second-guessing yourself. You're afraid that if you don't push hard enough, everything will collapse. That sound about right?"

Alex sighed. "Pretty much." Casey noticed that Alex's tense look started to relax. No one at Horizon Valley had ever acknowledged his feelings before.

She nodded as if that was what she had expected him to say. She paused before she said, "Resilience isn't about pushing through—it's about perspective. You have to decide what you're going to focus on."

He paused. "What do you mean?"

"If all you see is failure, all you'll feel is failure. The best leaders stay steady because they choose what they focus on. When everything is going wrong, they look for ways to be grateful."

Alex thought back to the meeting. There wasn't much to be grateful for, or at least it didn't feel like it.

"Gratitude builds resilience," Casey continued. "If you want your team to stay engaged, start by reminding them to be grateful. Leaders who focus on gratitude instead of what's failing create stronger, more engaged teams."

Alex crossed his arms. "So, I'm just supposed to tell them to be grateful?"

Casey shook her head. "That's not entirely what I'm saying. Many leaders get angry when goals or objectives get blocked. When someone on the team undermines plans and deadlines, it's easy to get angry. When we don't focus on joy and being grateful, anxiety and fear take control."

She stepped onto the curb. "Ever notice how the mood of a room shifts depending on the leader's energy?"

Alex knew what she was talking about. The moment Howard had walked in, the room had tightened. When Howard was angry, people shrank. When he was stressed, they panicked.

"Resilient teams feed off their leader's energy," Casey said. "If you're frantic, they will be, too. If you stay grounded, they follow suit."

Alex nodded, letting her words sink in. Then, he asked, "So, what, I just fake being calm?"

Casey smiled at him. "No. You practice it. And you start by shifting your focus to joy and gratitude."

She leaned in a little. "Notice what's working. Celebrate progress—even small wins. Speak hope out loud. It rewires your brain to see possibilities, not just problems."

Alex tilted his head, considering it. “Joy as strategy.”

“Exactly,” she said. “It’s not about pretending everything’s fine. It’s about choosing where you anchor your mindset.”

CASEY’S CRISIS STORY

Alex and Casey kept walking. Finally, she said, “You know, I used to lead like Howard.”

That got his attention.

Casey sighed as if the memory still carried weight. “There was this one project—high stakes, tight deadline, everything on the line. And we were struggling. People were exhausted, mistakes were piling up, and I could feel everything slipping.”

Alex knew that feeling.

“I panicked,” she admitted. “I started doing what Howard does—tightening the reins, pushing harder, getting frustrated when people didn’t meet expectations. I thought pressure would make them work faster. Instead, they shut down. Just like your team did today.”

Alex didn’t say anything. He didn’t need to.

Casey continued. “One of my top people—someone I trusted—pulled me aside and said, ‘Casey, we used to believe in what we were doing. Now, we’re just trying not to disappoint you.’ I carried those words with me for months. He transferred to another department two weeks later. I never got that trust back.”

She shook her head. "That hit me hard. Because he was right, they weren't failing—I was."

Alex looked down at the pavement, lost in thought. "So, what did you do?" he asked.

Casey smiled slightly. "I stopped trying to control everything. I started acknowledging effort instead of pointing out what wasn't done yet. I celebrated the small wins. Instead of saying 'we're behind,' I started saying 'we're making progress.'"

Alex raised an eyebrow. "And that was enough?"

Casey gave him a knowing look. "It was about keeping my team engaged enough to fix it together."

She turned toward him. "Resilience is forged in the storm—not after it."

Alex let out a slow breath, her words settling in. *Maybe resilience wasn't just pushing through—it's how you see the challenge and lead the team to do the same.*

APPLYING PURPOSEFUL RESILIENCE

Alex walked back into the office, the weight of missing the revenue and profit deadline pressing down on him. He could see it on his team's faces, too—shoulders tight, eyes glued to their screens, tension thick in the air. The same silence that had filled the bullpen earlier hung over them.

As the deadline loomed, Alex faced a critical decision. He could let the stress consume the team or take a different approach to re-engage them.

Taking a breath, he clapped his hands together. "Alright, Lisa, Mark, Jordan—let's huddle up."

A few heads lifted, hesitant. People exchanged glances, unsure if this was the beginning of another pressure-filled speech. Jordan sighed, arms crossed. "Alex, we don't have time for this."

"We don't have time not to," Alex countered. He motioned for them to gather. "Look, I know we're behind. I know this deadline feels impossible. But before we dive back in, I want to ask something." He scanned the group, making sure they were listening. "What's something that you are grateful for this week?"

They answered him with silence.

Lisa blinked at him. "What?"

Alex repeated himself. "One thing. Something you're grateful for."

There was another beat of hesitation. The expectation in the room was clear: Leaders should only point out problems and get them fixed.

Jordan scoffed. "This isn't the time for positivity. We need to work."

Alex nodded. "Yeah, we do. But working in a constant state of stress won't get us anywhere. We've been moving fast, fixing issues left and right—so let's take a second and recognize that."

Lisa shifted, still hesitant, then spoke. "Well, I am grateful we solved that scheduling issue yesterday."

Alex smiled, nodded, and affirmed. "Yeah, that was a big one."

Across the room, someone else added, "And we figured out the software problem." A murmur of agreement followed, then another voice, a little more confident this time: "And the client sent a follow-up this morning—no issues with the last rollout."

Alex felt it happen. It was fundamental—the shift from exhaustion to perspective. Their posture straightened just slightly. Instead of only seeing the stress, they were also seeing the progress. And that was the point.

Alex nodded, giving them a moment to absorb it. "We're not done yet, but let's build on what's already working."

The four broke apart, returning to their teams. But the silence that followed wasn't the same as before. It wasn't the tense, bracing-for-impact kind—it was the kind that came from focus and engagement.

Alex exhaled. Maybe Casey was onto something.

THE FIRE THAT BURNS OR BUILDS

Howard stood inside his office, arms crossed, watching. Alex had seen that look before. To Howard, pressure was necessary—without it, people got lazy.

He motioned to Alex to join him. When he finally spoke, his voice carried the same edge as when he was unimpressed, low but sharp. "This isn't summer camp, Alex. People don't need pep talks—they need a fire under them."

Alex didn't react immediately. The old instinct that wanted to seek approval from Howard flared up momentarily, but he pushed it aside. "I am trying to connect with everyone more."

Howard stopped and gave an intense look right into Alex's eyes. "Oh, so you're just trying to be everyone's favorite now? What, are you trying to win people over to your side?"

Alex met his gaze. "They're already working hard. What they need is to believe that effort is actually leading somewhere."

Howard smirked. "Well, of course, they're working hard—because of the vision I've set. Without leadership, all that effort would be pointless. They need to work hard because that's what they're paid to do—not because they need to feel good about it."

Alex could not believe this conversation was happening. It almost felt like he had become a spectator in the office. He had spent a long time watching Howard lead this way—constant pressure, constant demands, no acknowledgment of progress. And where had it gotten them? A team that worked out of fear, not joy or gratitude, a group of people who gave just enough to avoid being blamed but never enough to take ownership.

Howard's version of leadership was isolating. His presence didn't inspire people to succeed—it made them afraid of failure.

Resilience meant more than pushing through. It required embracing the process. It wasn't about forcing people to endure more stress, demands, and pressure. It was about shaping a team's mindset—helping them see challenges as something they could overcome, not something that would crush them. Howard didn't believe in that. But Alex did.

Without another word, Alex turned and walked back to his desk. He couldn't change Howard's mind, but he could change how his team experienced his leadership, and that was enough.

THE IMPACT OF PURPOSEFUL RESILIENCE

Over the next few days, Alex became more deliberate about his leadership approach. He didn't force positivity or gloss over challenges. Instead, gratitude and mindset became his focus. Small but steady shifts showed up in how he interacted with the team.

When someone solved a problem, he acknowledged it. When a mistake happened, he encouraged discussion instead of assigning blame. As tension rose, Alex pointed out the team's progress rather than dwelling on unfinished tasks.

At first, the changes were barely noticeable. The stress of the looming deadline remained, and the workload hadn't lessened. However, the team's energy was different.

People started engaging more. Instead of waiting for instructions, they proactively offered solutions. Instead of hesitating in meetings, they spoke up. Alex could see it in how they carried themselves—more focus, less dread.

One afternoon, Lisa turned to the group and, almost casually, said, "Well, at least we're past the worst of it. We actually got ahead of the revenue projections."

It was a simple comment, but Alex caught it. A week ago, she wouldn't have said that, and she wouldn't have been looking for anything positive.

Little by little, things were shifting. The workload was still demanding, but the team was handling it differently. They weren't just trying to survive the deadline. They were working toward it as a team.

DEADLINE DAY

When the deadline finally arrived, Alex wasn't sure what to expect. No amount of leadership shifts could erase the fact that they had been behind, and no encouragement could guarantee that everything would come together in time. But it did.

Despite the setbacks, Alex and his team exceeded the revenue and profit goals. They succeeded not because of pressure or fear but because they remained joyful and grateful. Lisa and Mark exceeded their goals.

As Alex watched his team pack up for the day, he could see their exhaustion, but it wasn't the kind that came from burnout. The team was tired but felt accomplished and happy to be together.

On the other side of the office, Jordan's team had also met the deadline, but there was no celebration—just exhausted silence and the rush to clock out.

Howard sat at his desk, arms crossed, trying not to look out the glass windows. His team had delivered. He was glad to report the progress and numbers to the CEO and executives.

Alex could feel Howard's frustration. It was not because the project had failed but because Alex had succeeded without doing it his way. Howard would never acknowledge it, but he didn't have to.

For the first time, Alex realized he wasn't looking for Howard's approval. He wasn't trying to match his leadership style or prove anything to anyone. He had led the way. And it worked. Moreover, it felt right.

Howard emailed everyone in his department.

Exceptional Results - A Testament to Our Vision

Alex
to everyone

Team,

I'm incredibly proud to announce that we've not only met but exceeded our CEO's revenue and profit goals—an achievement that reflects the standards of excellence I've always believed this team was capable of.

This milestone wouldn't have been possible without the guidance and strategic direction I've worked hard to instill over the past quarter. Watching you step up and execute our vision together has been truly inspiring.

While more work always lies ahead, this win proves that success comes from executing the plan and staying aligned with our priorities.

Thank you all for your hard work and dedication—I look forward to seeing how far we can go from here.

Let's keep the momentum going!

Howard

Resilience is a Mindset

The office had finally quieted down. Most of the team had left for the night, and Alex sat at his desk, trying to ignore the emptiness he felt as he tried to ignore Howard's email. The numbers confirmed what he already knew—the team had delivered. But that wasn't what was on his mind.

What stuck with him wasn't just the outcome but how they had gotten there. He had spent so much time thinking resilience meant pushing through, holding on, and surviving whatever came his way. But that wasn't it at all.

Resilience was about shifting how you saw the challenge. A burden could feel unbearable, or it could be a step forward. The choice made all the difference.

He had seen it happen in real time: the shift in his team's energy. They started to look for gratitude instead of external pressure. They carried themselves not as people scrambling to keep up but as a team that believed they could handle what was ahead. People tend to adopt their leader's energy. And it had started with him.

A familiar voice pulled him from his thoughts. "You survived."

Alex looked up to see Casey leaning against the doorframe, arms crossed, a slight smirk on her face. He let out a breath, shaking his head. "Barely."

She stepped inside, taking a seat across from him. "But you did more than survive."

Alex thought about that for a moment, then nodded. "Yeah. I think I did."

Casey studied him as if waiting for the realization to click. Then, with a knowing smirk, she asked, "So, what's the takeaway here?"

Alex exhaled, leaning back in his chair. "Resilience isn't just getting through the hard stuff—it's helping people believe they can. It's a mindset."

Casey smiled. "Now you're getting it." She stood up, stretching slightly. "You did well, Alex."

Alex nodded seriously. He had a feeling that was the case.

She gave him a knowing look. "Resilience is one thing. But what happens when things don't work out? When you do everything right and still fail?"

Alex sat up, the weight of that question settling over him.

Casey tapped the desk lightly as she turned to leave. "That's the next step in leadership—learning to navigate failure without losing momentum." She walked out, leaving Alex with that thought.

He wasn't sure he was ready for that lesson yet. But he had a feeling he'd be learning it soon enough.

REFLECT

1. This chapter taught Alex the importance of resilience, enduring pressure, and shaping a team's response to challenges. How do you typically react to high-pressure situations? Do you focus more on the problems or potential solutions?

2. Alex introduced gratitude and acknowledgment to keep his team engaged. How has recognition (or the lack of it) affected your experience in a team setting?

3. Alex struggled between his instinct to push harder and Casey's advice to shift perspective. Have you ever been caught between two opposing leadership styles? How did you handle it?

4. Casey said, "Resilient teams feed off their leader's energy." In what ways do you see this playing out in your own work or leadership experiences?

ACTION

1. Alex began practicing small, consistent habits of resilience, such as acknowledging wins, encouraging open discussions, and keeping the team focused on solutions. What small but impactful habits can you implement to strengthen resilience in your leadership?

2. Reflect on your emotional presence as a leader. Are you unintentionally adding to your team's stress or helping them find perspective?

3. Alex learned that people absorb the energy of their leader. When leading, consider the environment you create—are you promoting focus, confidence, stress, and uncertainty? What is one change you can make to reinforce a culture of stability?

4. Casey asked Alex, "What happens when you do everything right and still fail?" Reflect on a time you faced failure despite your best efforts. What did you learn from it? How did it shape your leadership approach?

5. What will you do to stay motivated and not lose momentum if something goes wrong in the future?

Dear Alex,

Resilience isn't about pushing through–it's about perspective. You have to decide what you're going to focus on.

Your Friend, Casey

CHAPTER 5

EMBRACING CHALLENGES

THE GROWTH OPPORTUNITY

Sometimes, the bravest thing you can do is tell someone, 'I need help.'"

–Dan Allender

A cold wind rattled against the tall windows, carrying the steady rhythm of rain hammering the glass. Gray clouds pressed low over the horizon, casting a dull, oppressive light into the room. The kind of day where the weather crept in from the outside, settled into your bones, heavy and unwelcome. The storm mirrored the tension building inside Alex. Some days didn't just bring pressure—they demanded a fight.

Anticipation filled the air inside Horizon Valley's conference room. The upcoming leadership review felt more like an ordeal than a simple meeting—the kind that made stomachs tighten and hands grip pens too tightly. Across the room, department heads sat in stiff silence, eyes flicking between their notes and the closed door, waiting for Howard to arrive.

Alex sat near the end of the long table, his notepad resting beneath his hand. The room was heavy with tension, but Alex's battle wasn't just with the silence but inside him. He'd been working hard to lead his way, focusing on connection and trust, but part of him still wondered if it was enough—if he was enough.

Maybe Howard was right. Leadership was about exerting pressure, maintaining control, and wielding unquestioned authority. His gaze drifted to Howard's seat at the head of the table. If Alex could just get this right, maybe Howard would finally see him as a leader. But at what cost?

Then, the door opened.

Howard stepped into the room, and the air seemed to tighten. He didn't need to raise his voice. His silence was enough to pull the air out of the room. Whatever happened next wouldn't be a conversation but a test.

Alex sat up a little straighter, instinctively tightening his grip on his notepad. He knew this routine well. At the leadership review, Howard would go down the list, meticulously reviewing every department's performance, and ensure that no one left the room feeling confident.

Howard settled into his seat at the head of the table and flipped open a folder. “Let’s get started.”

There was no welcome, no acknowledgment of effort, just a signal that it was time for everyone to prove themselves.

The meeting unfolded as usual. Department heads tiptoed through their reports, carefully choosing their words to avoid triggering Howard’s frustration. It never mattered. His primary focus was to find mistakes.

“You missed your numbers last quarter,” Howard said to one department leader without looking up from his notes. “Why?”

He hesitated, trying to frame a response that wouldn't make things worse. "There were some unexpected vendor delays. Let me explain."

Howard looked at him and said, "I'm not here for the excuses. I don't need reasons. I need results."

A flicker of defeat crossed his face as he nodded, making a quick note, probably to revise the numbers before next time.

The next department head received a similar response, and then the next. It was like a countdown in Alex's head, slowly ticking down.

Howard never raised his voice, never outright belittled anyone, but he didn't have to. He was calm, his disappointment cutting deep, not through yelling, but through the silence that made people second-guess their abilities.

Then, it was Alex's turn.

Howard leaned back in his chair and sighed, shaking his head before Alex spoke. "I don't understand you," he said. "You should be further along than this."

Alex clenched his jaw, biting back the urge to push back—what would be the point?

Howard closed his folder, his gaze steady but calm. "The challenge, Alex, is that you're still approaching this from your perspective. It's time to start seeing it from mine."

Alex steadied himself, keeping his face neutral. The words hit harder than he expected. He wasn't sure what frustrated him more—that Howard kept demanding this or that part of him still wanted to earn his approval.

Howard didn't notice the internal struggle. He was already moving on to the next person and the next criticism. The meeting continued, and the tension in the room was as thick as ever.

And Alex sat there, feeling all the weight pressing down on him.

The fallout lingered in the air like static. People moved through the office, not in panic—but in that quiet, uneasy rhythm that followed a mistake no one wanted to own out loud.

Alex sat at his desk, jaw tight, staring at his screen but seeing none of it. He hadn't said much since the incident. He wasn't even sure what there was to say.

Across the floor, Casey watched from a distance—not with judgment, but with recognition. She had seen this kind of silence before. It wasn't incompetence. It was culture doing exactly what it had been trained to do.

SAY MORE ABOUT THAT

The corner café inside the Horizon Valley office building was never silent. The hum of espresso machines, the occasional burst of laughter, and the murmur of quiet conversations were the closest thing to normal in a workplace that always seemed to be on edge.

But today, the energy was different. The usual background noise was present, but it seemed thinner and more forced. People spoke in hushed tones, as if waiting for something to go wrong.

That afternoon, as Casey walked by the café, she noticed Alex at a small table by the window. She watched him as he stared down at his phone, scrolling aimlessly. He wasn't reading anything. He wasn't texting anyone—he was just... there.

A few months ago, that wouldn't have been the case. Alex used to be engaged and present, always quick to share his opinions. Now, the weight on his shoulders was visible in how he barely reacted, refusing to admit how much it dragged him down.

She let her eyes drift across the café. At a nearby booth, Lisa and Jordan sat with their heads close together, their voices low but sharp with frustration.

Casey let out a quiet sigh. She had seen this before. She had seen what fear-based leadership did to people—how it hollowed them out, made them hesitate before speaking, and turned talented individuals into people who just wanted to get through the day without being called out.

Alex noticed her looking into the café. Nothing. No reaction. No shift in posture. No flicker of recognition. He was pulling away. And that worried her more than anything else. She sat down across from him. *This isn't leadership. This is fear.*

It wasn't just Alex. It was all of them. The entire company operated like a machine built on tension, running just well enough to keep moving but never well enough to thrive. Howard's leadership kept the company moving, but the people behind it ran on fumes.

She leaned forward slightly, keeping her voice steady. "You know, hardship in leadership is inevitable," she said. "But how you handle it determines your growth."

Alex blinked, finally looking up. "What?"

Casey tilted her head toward Lisa and Jordan. "That's not leadership," she said. "That's survival. And you're starting to look like them."

Alex frowned, rubbing the back of his neck. "I'm just tired."

Casey nodded. "I know. But there's a difference between being tired and being worn down."

He exhaled sharply, looking away. "It's just a rough patch."

"Maybe," Casey said, letting the moment pass before adding, "but rough patches don't make people withdraw. Fear does."

Alex's grip on his coffee tightened, and she knew she had hit something more profound than he was ready to admit.

"Pressure without guidance leads to burnout, not development," she continued. "Fear-based leadership doesn't build strong teams. It isolates people, making them too exhausted to lead. True leaders don't retreat under pressure—they stay connected, even when it's hard."

Alex didn't argue.

"You're not failing because things are hard," Casey said, her voice softer now. "You're struggling because you're carrying this all by yourself."

For a second, he didn't respond. He just sat there, staring at his cup like it held the answer to all of his problems. The swirl of coffee mirrored the chaos in his mind—endless, unsettled. His fingers tightened around the ceramic as if grounding himself in something solid could keep him from unraveling completely.

Then, finally, he let out a breath, slow and unsteady. "I think I'm losing myself a little," he admitted, his voice low, barely above a whisper. The words felt heavier than he expected, like they carried more truth than he was ready to face.

Casey nodded, her gaze steady but gentle. "Say more about that," she encouraged her tone calm but firm—an invitation, not a demand.

Alex's throat felt dry as he swallowed. "It's like I walk into this place, and I feel like a different person. I second-guess every word, every decision. I'm constantly wondering if I'm doing enough, being enough, or if I'm just one mistake away from losing everything." He glanced toward the window, watching the rain blur the view. "I used to know who I was here. I used to feel confident. Now, it's like I'm shrinking. Every time I try to lead, I wonder if I'm doing it wrong."

Casey didn't interrupt. She let the silence hold, a space where the truth could settle.

Alex looked back at her, his jaw tight. "I don't even recognize myself some days. I come home, and I feel like I've left half of me behind. The part that believes I can actually do this." He shook his head, his voice rougher now. "I'm tired of pretending it's fine when it's not."

Casey's expression softened, her voice low. "That's not losing yourself, Alex. That's seeing the cracks for the first time. And it's the first step to figuring out how to put the pieces back together."

He looked at her, searching for something in her words—hope, maybe, or just the belief that he wasn't beyond repair.

AT THE BREAKING POINT

Howard's office had a way of making people feel small. The towering bookshelves and the sleek, oversized desk seemed to absorb sound, leaving nothing but the weight of expectation.

Alex stood in front of the desk, project folder in hand, waiting as Howard flipped through the pages. The silence stretched as Alex waited.

Howard finally exhaled, shaking his head in disbelief. He didn't look up. "This is what you came up with?"

Alex tightened his grip on the folder. "I—yeah. I based it on the last quarter's numbers and projected adjustments based on client behavior."

Howard was calm as he placed the folder on the desk, his gaze lingering on Alex with a weight that felt heavier than words. "And that's the problem. You based it on what you think will happen. It is your responsibility to be ahead of the game, you have to dictate what you want to happen."

The words slid across the table like a quiet accusation, cloaked in calm but sharp beneath the surface. Alex held his posture, but something twisted in his chest. His perspective. It was as if something in him was inherently flawed—as if the way he viewed the team, the project, and leadership itself needed fixing.

Howard leaned back, folding his arms with measured patience. "You're still playing it safe. Still thinking small. You're focused on what's in front of you instead of seeing the bigger game." He paused, letting the silence add weight to his words. "Leadership isn't about staying comfortable. It's about stepping beyond what feels safe and knowing when to push harder. If you can't do that, you'll always be two steps behind."

Howard didn't speak in anger. He used the calm, dismissive tone he always reserved for those he saw as uncertain.

Alex fought to keep his expression neutral, but the words sank deeper than he wanted to admit. It wasn't just his approach, Howard questioned—it felt personal, as if Alex himself wasn't enough.

Still, he said nothing. Arguing wouldn't change anything.

Howard's gaze didn't waver. "You've got potential, Alex. But potential isn't leadership. Vision and results are what ultimately matter. And until you start seeing things the right way, you'll keep missing the mark."

Alex felt his jaw tighten as Howard let out a sigh. "If I have to keep cleaning up after you, this isn't going to work."

That was it. There was no direction, no real feedback, just a vague, sweeping dismissal. The expectation hung over Alex, but he had no idea what Howard wanted.

Alex nodded slowly, but the agreement felt hollow. Howard seemed satisfied, though. He always was when the conversation ended his way. Alex stood, the weight of the conversation settling over him like a shadow he couldn't shake.

ALEX EMBRACES CHALLENGE

Back at his desk, Alex opened his laptop and stared at the project outline as Howard's words echoed in his head. *"You don't think like a leader."* The cursor blinked.

His fingers hovered over the keyboard. The numbers were right in front of him. The plan was already forming in his head. And yet, he couldn't move.

Taking the initiative meant stepping into Howard's line of fire—he would tear apart the approach and call it a failure. Asking for clarity would be seen as a weakness. Making the wrong call would only prove Howard right. So, instead, Alex sat there, trapped between choices that all led to failure.

"You've been staring at that for 10 minutes." Lisa's voice cut through the fog.

Alex blinked, looking up to see her leaning against his desk, arms crossed.

"What's up?" she asked.

He hesitated. "I just... I just don't know anymore. I can't seem to do anything right."

Lisa studied him for a second before pulling up a chair. "That's the problem," she said. "You're trying to be Howard. You don't lead like him, and you shouldn't. You're sitting here trying to make the 'right' decision when you already know what to do."

Alex exhaled sharply, rubbing the back of his neck. "If I do it my way, he's going to tell me it's wrong."

Lisa sighed. "Maybe. But does that mean you give up?"

She smiled. "Look, I get it. But Howard's not the only one who matters. Your team needs a leader, not a copy of him. I've seen you trying things differently, and it works."

Alex tapped his fingers against the desk, gazing at the screen once more.

"Real leaders don't copy—they connect," Lisa said. "Isolation feeds doubt. Stay with your team."

Alex leaned back in his chair. "So, what—just ignore Howard?"

Lisa shook her head. "No. But stop trying to meet expectations that keep shifting. Lead how you lead."

The words settled. After avoiding mistakes for so long, actual leadership had taken a backseat. That had to change.

Alex stood before his team an hour later, hands resting on the table as he scanned the room. This project wasn't a one-person job—he knew that. The real question was whether he would take the lead or wait for someone else to make the decision.

Howard's voice crept into his thoughts. *"You need to think like me. You think too small."*

Alex straightened. "Alright," he said, clapping his hands together. "We need to break this down. Lisa, what are the key priorities?"

Without hesitation, Lisa answered with a small smile, "Client retention and damage control."

Alex nodded. "Perfect. Let's divide and conquer." His voice was steady, though a ripple of uncertainty stirred beneath the surface.

Some team members exchanged wary glances, their stiff postures betraying their unease. Eyes flicked toward the door, as if expecting Howard to walk in at any moment and dismantle everything with a single sharp comment. The shadow of his presence lingered, an unspoken fear pressing against the edges of the room.

But not everyone looked afraid. Some team members weren't watching the door—they were watching Alex. They weren't just waiting for instructions. They were looking for certainty—for permission to believe this approach wouldn't collapse under pressure.

Lisa gave the slightest nod of approval, a small but deliberate show of support. It wasn't loud, but it was enough. Mark sat forward, his lips parted like he was considering speaking up, but unsure if now was the time. Even Jordan, who rarely stepped into leadership conversations, seemed less guarded, his arms uncrossing as he leaned in slightly.

It wasn't unanimous. Not yet. Fear still lingered—of mistakes, failure, and what would happen if they backed the wrong leader. But Alex saw something else, too. It was a question in their eyes—a question they didn't know how to ask, but were waiting for him to answer: *Are we safe to trust you?*

It wasn't much. But it was a start. Alex took a breath, letting the silence settle before speaking again. Not rushed. Not forced. Just steady.

"We know what's in front of us," he said, meeting each gaze. "And we know what we're capable of. Let's focus on that."

Another pause. Another small shift. Lisa's shoulders relaxed, Mark's fingers tapped nervously against his notebook, but he didn't look away. Jordan gave the faintest nod.

Alex felt it then—not a victory, but the edge of something more substantial than fear—trust, still fragile but forming.

He wasn't Howard. And that felt like a good thing for the first time in a while.

ALEX TURNS TO HIS TEAM

Alex kept leading, though he could feel Howard's presence like a shadow draped over the room, heavy and watching. Every word, every decision, felt like it carried twice the weight, but he pressed on. He focused on his team—on their eyes, their posture, their subtle cues. They followed his direction, dividing tasks and aligning on priorities. It wasn't perfect. There were stumbles and moments of hesitation, but they were engaged. Present.

And then, something unexpected happened.

As they worked through a complex issue, Mark cracked a quiet joke—one of those dry comments that might have slipped by unnoticed any other day. But Lisa chuckled, and Jordan smirked. Alex caught it, that brief flicker of ease, and for the first time in what felt like weeks, the tension in the room loosened just slightly.

The team began to lean in, not just to the task, but to one another. Suggestions came more quickly, and conversations were less guarded. Laughter, hesitant at first, but then genuine, punctuated the discussion. It wasn't loud or disruptive, but it was real.

For the first time in a long time, they weren't just coworkers bound by deadlines. They were a team, enjoying the process, enjoying being together.

Alex felt it, a warmth threading through the cold weight that Howard's shadow had cast. He didn't interrupt the flow. He didn't force it. He just let it happen, encouraging where he could,

Back at their desks, the energy was different. Subtle, but undeniable. There wasn't the usual scramble to fix mistakes or the tense glances exchanged in anticipation of another round of criticism. What changed wasn't the workload. It was the pressure. Fear no longer pressed down on them, and the air felt lighter as a result.

Lisa leaned against a cubicle, arms crossed, her gaze steady on Alex. "You don't have to be Howard," she said, her voice quiet but sure. It wasn't a suggestion. It was permission.

Alex exhaled, running a hand over his face, the weight of those words settling over him. He wasn't sure if it was relief or fear. Maybe both.

Jordan, still typing at his desk, didn't look up, but his voice carried confidence. "Yeah, man. You led us well. That's what matters."

The simplicity of the words caught Alex off guard. No pretense. No hesitation. Just the truth.

Alex sat down heavily, his fingers tapping against the desk in a slow rhythm. For months, leadership had felt like chasing shadows—an endless game of trying to meet expectations that were always just out of reach. He had convinced himself that leadership meant mastering Howard's formula. If he could think like Howard, act like Howard, maybe he'd finally get it right. Maybe then, Howard would see him—approve of him.

But now? Maybe leadership wasn't about surviving under someone else's shadow. Maybe it wasn't about approval at all. Perhaps it was about trusting his instincts, leading from his convictions, even if it meant walking a path Howard wouldn't understand.

Maybe it wasn't about proving himself to Howard but about proving to himself that he could lead differently—and that it could still be enough. And maybe, that was the only approval that mattered.

And then, a notification popped up on his screen.

Alex didn't need to guess what this was about.

CHAPTER 5

WHAT IF HE'S RIGHT?

Alex found himself inside Howard's office for the second time that day. The air felt colder here, the sleek furniture and towering bookshelves casting long, silent shadows. Howard sat behind his desk, composed and unreadable, the weight of expectation hanging heavy in the space between them.

"You think you're ready to lead?" Howard asked, his voice calm but sharp, like a blade disguised in silk. The words weren't a question. They were a test, like he already had the answer.

Alex kept his posture straight, though the question struck deeper than he wanted to admit. "I just—I handled it the best way I could," he said, but even as the words left his mouth, they sounded thin, uncertain.

Howard leaned back, a slow smirk playing at the corners of his mouth. "Your way?" He let the words linger, heavy and suffocating. "Alex, you really don't understand, do you?" He shook his head, as if disappointed in a child who hadn't learned a simple lesson. "You think this is about effort? About trying your best? That's not leadership. That's survival."

Alex felt the sting, his stomach twisting. He could hear Howard's unsaid words. He'd heard of it many times. "Things had to be done his way."

Howard studied him, waiting for some submission—some sign that Alex understood who was in control, but Alex said nothing.

Howard's voice softened, almost pitying. "Look, I get it. You're doing what you think is right. But let me be clear—you've been lucky so far. Your team's performance? It's not because of your leadership. It's because they're scared of failing me. Scared of losing their jobs." He paused, letting the implication settle. "And you should be, too."

The words lodged deep, the room shrinking around Alex.

Howard stood and walked around the desk, his tone gentle but cutting. "I'm not trying to be harsh. I'm trying to help you. You're not there yet, Alex. You still think small and naive—safe, hesitant. And I need a leader who can think big."

Alex's jaw tightened, but he stayed quiet.

Howard tilted his head, studying him with mock concern. "Do you even realize how often I've had to step in and clean up your mistakes? And not just yours but your team's. If I weren't constantly fixing things behind the scenes, you wouldn't be here anymore."

Alex blinked, caught off guard. It wasn't true. He knew it wasn't true. But Howard said it with such calm certainty that it made him question his memory. Had Howard been fixing things? Was Alex missing something?

Howard leaned in slightly. "I'm protecting you, Alex. Even when you don't see it, but I can't keep covering for you forever. Sooner or later, the higher-ups will start asking questions. And I can only protect people who make my job easier, not harder."

It was a threat and an ultimatum wrapped in false concern.

Howard stepped back, smiling faintly. "I say this because I believe you could be a leader. If you'd just stop resisting and start thinking like me."

Alex's pulse hammered in his ears. He wanted to speak, to defend himself, but his words stuck. Doubt pressed in, suffocating him. *What if Howard was right? What if all his progress with the team was just an illusion? What if his way was the wrong way?*

Howard watched him, calm and assured, like a man who had already won. "I'm not trying to push you down, Alex. I'm trying to lift you up. You just have to let me."

The words were a trap, but they were also comforting. Easy. Safe.

Alex braced himself, the weight of uncertainty pressing against his chest. Maybe this was the cost of leadership—letting go of who he thought he was to become the leader Howard demanded. Perhaps that was the only way to survive here.

But then, a flicker of another voice cut through the fog. Lisa's earlier words: "You don't have to be Howard." And Jordan's steady encouragement: *"You led us well. That's what matters."*

Alex looked up. Howard's smile hadn't wavered, but there wasn't concern behind his eyes. It was control. And Alex finally saw it for what it was.

"I hear you," Alex said quietly. He didn't fight or push back. Not yet.

The silence stretched between them. Finally, Alex gave a slight nod.

Howard was satisfied with that. "Good. Now, go fix it."

Alex turned and left the office, but every step felt heavier than the last. The words clung to him, sharp and suffocating.

Back at his desk, he sat motionless, his hands hovering over his keyboard. Doubt circled like a shadow. Maybe Howard was right. *Maybe everything Alex had tried was already crumbling.*

But then, why did his team trust him? Why had they engaged when he led the way? Howard had planted the seed of doubt, but Alex wasn't sure it would take root. Not yet.

And maybe—just maybe—he wasn't as broken as Howard wanted him to believe.

Buried, Not Broken

The conference room was dark, shadows pooling in the corners, broken only by the dim glow of Alex's laptop screen. The soft hum of the computer was the only sound, a lonely rhythm in an office long since emptied. Everyone else had gone home hours ago, leaving behind empty chairs and abandoned coffee mugs. But Alex hadn't moved.

He wasn't working. Not really. His eyes flicked over the same paragraphs again and again, scrolling through the document without absorbing a single word. It was as if the words were blurred, lost beneath the weight pressing down on him.

His body felt heavy, every muscle thick with exhaustion. But his mind felt heavier still. Clogged with the weight of expectations, silent criticisms, and endless pressure to measure up. It wasn't just today. It wasn't just this week. It was months and months of trying to keep pace, of proving himself, of surviving under Howard's shadow. And tonight, it had all caught up to him.

He could feel it, like a tightness in his chest, like gravity had doubled its hold on his shoulders. The air felt thick, his thoughts heavier still.

When the door opened, he didn't look up. The soft click of the handle felt intrusive, unwelcome. However, the footsteps that followed were light and measured. Familiar. Casey.

Casey didn't speak right away. She stepped inside quietly, her presence calm and patient. She didn't need to ask why Alex was still there. She already knew.

She pulled out a chair and sat across from him, resting her arms lightly on the table. She didn't fill the silence, didn't offer advice or comfort that felt too soon. She simply waited, her posture open but steady, offering presence instead of words.

It wasn't silence meant to pressure. It was silence meant to hold space. And somehow, that made it feel safer.

The room was heavy with silence, the kind that settled deep in the bones, stretching between them like an unsaid truth. The soft glow of the laptop illuminated the fatigue etched into Alex's face, shadows sinking into the hollows beneath his eyes.

Finally, Casey spoke, her voice low but steady. "You okay?"

Alex let out a tired chuckle, though there was no humor in it. It was hollow, forced. "Define 'okay.'"

Casey tilted her head, studying Alex—not with judgment, but with the kind of understanding that comes from experience. She wasn't asking about tasks, deadlines, or progress updates. She was asking about Alex himself.

When she spoke, her words were quiet but sharp. "A leader who makes you doubt yourself isn't mentoring you, Alex. They're breaking you."

Alex's exhale was long, as if the words released something he hadn't admitted until now. "That's exactly what it feels like." His voice cracked slightly at the end, but he didn't correct it.

He rubbed his hands together as if trying to shake off the weight that had settled into his skin. His gaze dropped to the table, tracing the grain of the wood like it could give him the courage to speak the words that followed.

"I don't even know if I belong here anymore." The words slipped out, raw and unfiltered. He didn't mean to say the words, but once they left his mouth, they lingered—heavier than he expected.

Casey didn't react. She didn't offer hollow reassurances or reach for easy comfort—just nodded, her eyes steady, patient. She knew better than to interrupt what needed to come to the surface.

Alex stopped, his thoughts racing. "I used to love this job. I used to be excited about leading." He paused, pressing his palms flat against the table, his hands tense. "But now? I don't even know who I am when I'm here."

The confession burned. For Alex, it felt like stripping away a layer of armor he had worn for too long—the kind that protected him but also kept him from breathing freely.

"I feel like I'm unraveling," he admitted, his voice no louder than a whisper. And that was the truth. Not that he was breaking under the deadlines or the pressure, but under the slow, silent erosion of himself.

Casey nodded, but her gaze softened. There was understanding there, but also something more—resolve. "Then it may be time to stop trying to hold everything together yourself."

Alex let out a slow breath, his fingers rubbing against his temple as if trying to hold the thoughts inside his head in place. But they were slipping, scattering. He had spent so long convincing himself that leadership meant carrying it all, holding it all, pushing through even when every part of him screamed to stop. If he just worked harder, pushed faster, figured out the right formula, he could hold it together.

But now? The truth was undeniable. He wasn't holding anything together. He was barely holding himself together.

"I think I need help," he said, though the words felt like sand on his tongue. Weak. Exposed. But real. "But I don't know. I don't feel confident in any part of my life. I don't even know where to start."

He hated how raw it sounded, how much it revealed, but he was too tired to care anymore.

Casey didn't move for a moment, didn't rush to fill the space with comfort. When she finally spoke, her voice was firm but laced with empathy.

"Part of leadership," she said softly, "is knowing how to embrace challenges. And that doesn't mean ignoring the struggle or pushing harder until you break. It means knowing how to return to what grounds you. To joy. To be yourself."

Her gaze didn't waver. "It means knowing when you need help—and asking for it before the damage becomes too deep to fix."

Alex looked at her, his chest tightening. "But what if I don't know who I am here anymore? What if I've already lost that?"

"You haven't," Casey said gently. "You've just buried it under fear and pressure. It's still there. You just have to be willing to dig for it."

He shook his head slightly, glancing down at his hands. "It feels too far gone."

"It's not," she said, and her certainty was unwavering. "But it won't come back on its own."

She hesitated, choosing her words carefully. "You need someone outside of this—someone who can help you sort through it."

Alex tried to process the meaning behind her words, knowing they were hitting their mark. "You mean therapy?"

Casey nodded. "Yes." She leaned in slightly, her voice lower, steadier. "Because this isn't just about leadership, Alex. It's about you. It's about getting back to the parts of yourself that you've been pushing aside just to survive."

He opened his mouth, but nothing came out.

"And before you tell me that asking for help makes you weak," she added, "I'll remind you—it doesn't. It proves you're a leader. Because the strongest leaders know when they've reached their limit. And they know how to take the next step anyway."

Alex's throat felt thick. The idea of asking for help, of admitting how close he was to breaking, felt like stepping into open air. But what terrified him more was what would happen if he didn't.

He nodded, the movement small but certain.

"I think you're right," he said, though the words barely felt like his own.

Casey's expression softened, but she didn't let the moment go. "You're stronger than you think. But you don't have to prove that by breaking yourself to hold everything together."

Alex exhaled, long and shaky, the weight of the truth heavy but honest. For the first time, he wasn't just thinking about change. He wasn't fantasizing about relief. He was ready to take the first step.

Reflect

1. How do you recognize when external expectations (like Howard's) are shaping your leadership approach in negative ways?
2. Alex struggled with a fear of failure. How do you personally recognize when fear is influencing your deci-

sions? What small signs in a leader's behavior reveal emotional exhaustion?

3. Howard used control as a form of guidance and mentorship. How can you distinguish between constructive feedback and toxic critique in leadership?

4. Casey said, "True leaders don't retreat under pressure—they stay connected." When have you retreated in leadership, and how can you stay connected next time? What can help you stay connected with others?

5. Alex admitted he felt like he was unraveling. How do you protect your mental and emotional well-being when leadership pressures escalate? Why is asking for help often framed as failure in leadership cultures?

6. Alex's decision to seek therapy marks strength, not weakness. How can vulnerability be a leadership strength in your context? How can you evaluate whether your leadership approach is empowering or isolating those you lead?

ACTION

1. What's one thing you can do this week to make your team feel safer expressing challenges and setbacks?

2. When was the last time you admitted uncertainty to your team? How can you model that vulnerability this week?

3. How can you create more opportunities for your team to support one another, like Casey did for Alex?

4. The next time you feel pressure rising, what will you do to pause and respond thoughtfully instead of reacting impulsively? What are the early signs of burnout that you can look for in yourself or your team? How will you address them proactively?

5. Make a list of three signs that indicate when you're reaching your limit. Who can you talk to when you notice them?

Alex,

Part of leadership is knowing how to embrace challenges. And that doesn't mean ignoring the struggle or pushing harder until you break. It means knowing how to return to what grounds you. To joy. To being yourself.

-Casey

CHAPTER 6

BREAKING FREE

RECOVERING FROM TOXIC LEADERSHIP

Therapy isn't weakness-it's wisdom. The leader who knows when to ask for help leads others to do the same."

-Dr. Henry Cloud

The carpet muted Alex's footsteps as he stepped into the therapy office—soft earth tones and natural light spilled across the hardwood floor. A small couch sat near the window, not pressed stiffly against the wall but angled like it had been placed there by someone who understood comfort. Everything about the space felt intentional and unfamiliar.

He paused just past the threshold, eyes scanning the room. A bookshelf held a few well-worn titles, and a ceramic mug with a chipped handle rested on the desk. A small diffuser sent out a slow curl of lavender into the air. Nothing about it screamed productivity. No one had pinned timelines to the walls, set up glaring monitors, or stuffed folders with red-inked corrections.

It felt quiet, in a way his world rarely allowed. He stood frozen for a beat longer than he meant to. Then, it hit him: He didn't know what to do in a space like this. There was nothing to fix. No one to manage. No pressure to anticipate. Just breathe. And that felt strange. Maybe even unsafe.

"Hi, Alex," said a voice, warm and unhurried.

Carol stood across the room. She had no clipboard, lanyard, or air of evaluation—just a soft smile and a calm stillness that made the room feel even quieter.

"You can sit anywhere you'd like."

Alex nodded and went to the couch, slowly lowering himself like he wasn't sure he'd stay long. He leaned forward slightly, hands clasped between his knees. The silence wasn't uncomfortable yet.

Carol sat in a chair across from him, angled slightly, not directly opposite to him. She didn't fill the silence. Didn't ask the first question.

She just sat. Present. At ease.

"I'm not really sure how this goes," Alex said.

Carol nodded gently. "Most people don't." Her voice didn't carry expectations. "There's no script. No right way to start."

Alex nodded but didn't speak. His throat tightened as he shifted in his seat, eyes tracing the rug's weave as if it held instructions. The usual guard—that mix of careful phrasing and mental calculation he wore in meetings—still clung to him. But it was beginning to itch.

Carol sat still, her hands resting lightly on the chair's arms. One thumb slowly traced the seam of the cushion—grounded, calm, not rushed, not waiting for a performance. "Sometimes, it helps to start with what brought you here today."

Alex hesitated, his gaze dropping. "I guess I'm just tired."

Her expression didn't change. She didn't jump in or try to solve it. She let the word hang there a second longer before speaking.

"What kind of tired?" she asked.

He looked up briefly, then looked away. He gave a shallow shrug. "I'm not even sure anymore."

Carol nodded, no judgment behind her eyes. "What thoughts are contributing to this feeling?" Silence followed—thin but breathable.

"I work in a place where... I don't know. Things are tense. The kind of tense that doesn't go away just because the meeting ends," Alex said. "I used to think if I just tried hard enough, I could push through it. Be what everyone needed. But lately, I don't even know what that means."

Carol leaned back slightly. "Sounds like you've been operating under a lot of pressure."

Alex gave a short laugh, though there was no humor in it. "Pressure, yeah. And second-guessing. And trying to meet expectations, I'm not even sure if they're real."

Carol's voice stayed calm. "Where do you think that pressure is coming from?"

Alex sat with that for a moment, then nodded slowly. "It's not just the workload—it's the way everything runs through my boss, Howard. He sets the tone, and it's all pressure and perfection. There's no room for questions, just expectations that keep shifting. You mess up once, and it's like the trust resets to zero. Everyone walks on eggshells. You learn to adapt, not lead."

JORDAN UNDER PRESSURE

The office had been humming with something unspoken lately: a few closed-door meetings, a shift in the tone of department heads. Nobody said anything outright, but everyone felt it. Something was coming.

The blinds in Howard's office were half-drawn, casting harsh stripes of light across the floor. The overhead bulbs buzzed faintly, adding to the uneasy stillness in the room.

Jordan stood across from the desk, back stiff, hands tucked behind him to hide his fidgeting. Howard flipped through a thin stack of reports in silence, the sound of turning pages somehow louder than it should have been.

Jordan tried not to stare at the expressionless face across from him—tried not to anticipate the moment it would shift from bored disinterest to sharp criticism. He already knew what was coming. That was the worst part. It wasn't a surprise he feared, but the inevitability.

Howard finally set the papers down and looked into his eyes. "Jordan," Howard said, pausing just long enough to let the silence tighten, "this doesn't look like the work of someone who's aiming higher."

He flipped another page. "It's just not strategic. Alex understood how to anticipate what matters."

The comparison didn't need an explanation. Jordan had heard it before—maybe not in those exact words, but close enough. He opened his mouth to respond, something defensive halfway to the surface, but it caught in his throat.

His stomach churned, and a thin layer of sweat prickled under his collar. It was like standing too close to a speaker blaring static—nothing loud, but everything wrong.

What was he supposed to say? Was the team stretched thin? That things were fine until Howard changed the expectations without warning?

He blinked and gave a slight nod instead. Retreating felt easier than resisting.

Howard leaned back, satisfied with the silence. "You need to start acting like someone who takes this seriously."

Jordan stayed still. His palms itched with frustration, but he kept them hidden.

The meeting ended with no further instructions—just a wave of dismissal and a scribbled note on a yellow pad. Jordan nodded again and stepped out into the hallway, a strange mix of numbness and heat rising beneath his skin.

Down the corridor, his steps echoed more than usual. Or maybe he was just noticing them now.

He didn't head straight back to his desk. He paused momentarily near the breakroom, leaned against the wall, arms crossed, eyes unfocused. His chest felt tight—not like panic, not precisely—more like being cornered by something you couldn't name.

He thought about what Howard had said. About Alex. Howard used one person's performance to cut another down easily. And he hated how much it worked—how fast doubt crept in once someone said the words out loud.

Why did Howard's approval still matter so much?

He'd asked himself that question before. Never aloud, but quietly—usually in those empty moments between meetings. He told himself it was about growth, about rising to expectations. But deep down, he knew better. It wasn't growth but survival.

He needed Howard's approval like a shield. And when it slipped, so did everything else.

He closed his eyes, jaw tight. The pressure didn't fade it calcified. Not panic, not anger. Just a deep, dragging weight of someone else's disappointment and no map for setting it down.

And yet, somewhere beneath the heat in his chest, a feeling stirred. Maybe this wasn't just about Howard anymore. Perhaps it was about what kind of leader he was becoming.

CHAPTER 6

SPEAKING THE QUIET TRUTH

The second session felt different—not easier—just more familiar. Alex sat back on the couch, one ankle resting over his knee, his hands fidgeting with a seam on the cushion's fabric. Carol sat across from him, the same quiet presence, the notebook still untouched on her lap.

He exhaled slowly. "I think I've gotten used to tuning myself out."

Carol raised an eyebrow, inviting him to go on. As Alex spoke, Carol's fingers lightly traced the grain of the armrest. Not absent-minded, but attentive—like she was grounding herself as he unraveled.

"I mean—at work, I spend so much time adjusting. Reading the room. Reading Howard. Figuring out what version of me will get through the day without setting anything off." He paused, chewing on the edge of a thumbnail. "That's not something I used to do. I used to have a sense of who I was."

"There was a time when I could walk into a room and not brace myself," he said. "I used to lead meetings without rehearsing every line in my head. I'd crack a dumb joke. People would laugh. Not because they had to—because the room felt open."

Carol nodded. "And now?"

Alex leaned back. "Now, it's like I've been shrinking. Little by little. I still show up and make decisions, but I'm not leading. Not in a way that feels like mine. It's like I've been erasing little parts of myself to make room for what Howard needed. And now, I don't know what's left—just outlines and edits."

The statement had no dramatic swell—just a quiet resignation like he was describing something he'd finally admitted to himself.

Carol leaned in slightly. "You mentioned earlier that you've been 'shrinking.' What does that mean to you?"

Alex let the word hang in the air for a beat. "It's like I've stopped taking up space. I still show up, make decisions, get things done—but it's not really me leading. I'm more focused on avoiding mistakes than actually guiding anyone."

Carol nodded thoughtfully. "And what happens when you make a mistake? How do you usually respond?"

Alex gave a quiet laugh, not amused. "I brace. I immediately start thinking about how to fix it—or how to explain it before Howard can say anything. Criticism isn't feedback. It's fuel for silence, or worse—comparison."

Carol kept her tone even. "And when the approval does come, is it clear? Or does it feel unpredictable?"

Alex hesitated. "Depends. And when it happens, it's usually tied to metrics, not effort. You never know if something was truly good or just temporarily acceptable."

Carol let that sit for a moment before asking, "So, how do you navigate that?"

Alex's expression tightened. "That's the problem. I don't think I have been. I've been making choices based on how to stay out of Howard's line of sight—how not to get it wrong—instead of leading with what I believe is right."

Carol nodded gently. "That's what fear can do. It distorts our internal compass—makes us chase approval instead of clarity. You start to equate survival with success."

Alex looked down, thoughtful. "And in doing that, I think I lost track of what I stand for."

Carol rested her elbow on the arm of her chair. "Do you remember what it feels like to be grounded?"

Alex sat with the question for a moment, eyes unfocused. "I think I was more clear-headed. I didn't question every instinct. I didn't second-guess myself just because someone raised an eyebrow."

He paused again, voice quieter now. "But now, I overthink everything. Even stuff I know I'm good at. And I catch myself waiting for Howard's response before deciding if something went well."

She nodded, still listening. "That's internalized criticism. Over time, it becomes automatic—so much so that it feels like part of your own thinking. But it isn't."

Alex looked over, and something in his shoulders dropped—less tension, more recognition.

"I can see where I have been working—from a place of fear," he said. "Even when I tell myself I'm leading."

"That's something we can work with," Carol said. "Fear doesn't disqualify you from being a leader. It just makes the job harder when it goes unacknowledged."

"I don't want to believe it's fear," he said, shaking his head. "I've worked hard. I've led projects. I've kept people moving."

Carol nodded. "I'm sure you have. But effort born from fear often looks like strength—until it doesn't feel like you anymore."

Alex gave a slight nod, less confident than before—but maybe a little more honest with himself. "I didn't realize how loud the fear had gotten," he said quietly. "But I think I'm starting to hear myself again—just a little."

Rebuilding from the Inside

Alex leaned back slightly, his gaze fixed on the soft patterns in the rug between them. "There's something Casey said that's been sitting with me," he murmured.

Carol waited patiently.

"She told me that leadership isn't about pushing through pressure—it's about coming back to what grounds you. To joy, even."

He gave a slight shrug. "At the time, I nodded like I understood. But I don't think I got it until recently."

Carol offered a quiet prompt. "What do you think she meant?"

Alex took a breath, considering. "I think she meant there has to be something more than just surviving the day—something steady underneath all the noise. And I haven't been leading from that place. I've been reacting. Trying to avoid missteps. Trying to meet expectations that never stay the same."

He paused. "That's not the kind of leader I wanted to be."

Carol tilted her head. "So, what kind did you want to be?"

He let the question linger. Then, with quiet honesty, he said: "One that people trust. Someone who listens. Someone who stays calm when things get hard. I used to think I could be that person."

"You still can," Carol said. "What I am hearing you say is that the kind of leadership you want to show doesn't come from controlling outcomes. It comes from knowing what matters to you—and being willing to lead from that, even when it feels risky."

Alex nodded slowly in agreement.

"Let me ask you," she continued, "when have you felt like yourself as a leader?"

The question took him off guard. He glanced upward, weighing the question.

"There was a moment," he said. "Everyone looked tired—and defensive. Lisa had her arms crossed. Jordan wouldn't make eye contact. Normally, I would've jumped in—laid out a new plan, filled the silence. But instead, I just asked Lisa what we needed to focus on. And then, I shut up and let her answer."

He gave a half smile, faint but real. "It worked. Not because I had all the answers, but because I didn't try to act like I did. But it's strange. That meeting went better than any I've led in a while. Part of me still kept waiting for someone to say I was doing it wrong."

Carol nodded. "And how did that feel, knowing it worked?"

"Natural," he said. "Lighter."

Carol responded, "Was that moment joyful?"

Surprised, Alex thoughtfully said, "Not in a big way. But yeah. There was something right about it. Like I remembered why I wanted to lead in the first place."

She leaned forward slightly. "What would it look like to lead like that tomorrow?"

Pausing, Alex stated, "I think I'll ask more questions. Listen first. Even if it's uncomfortable."

Alex let that settle in. "I keep thinking confidence will come once I get it right," he said. "But maybe it's something I have to lead with, not wait for."

Carol smiled.

Weight of Boundaries Unset

Jordan stared at the screen before him, though he wasn't reading. The numbers blurred together, a spreadsheet with no end in sight. Around him, papers sat in uneven stacks—some urgent, some overdue, all demanding attention he didn't have to give. It felt like standing ankle-deep in rising water. No one else seemed to notice, but he was soaked—and sinking.

Another task, courtesy of Howard, landed in his inbox 20 minutes ago. There was no explanation, just a short subject line.

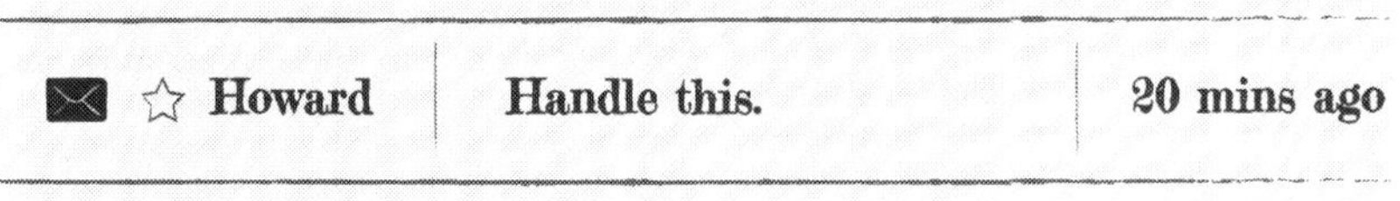

He didn't even blink anymore when those messages came through.

With Alex out, the load had shifted and landed hard on Jordan. Tasks piled up faster, and Howard's critical attention, once mostly reserved for Alex, now found a new target. Jordan had become the next focus, the next measuring stick, the next disappointment.

Jordan didn't push back. He kept saying yes, hoping that staying ahead of the next demand might shield him from the worst. He felt a tightness build behind his eyes. Reaching for his coffee, he set it back down untouched.

He'd told himself it was temporary. That stepping up would prove something. But whatever he was proving never seemed to matter. The tasks just kept coming. And he kept accepting them.

The noise of the office carried on—phones ringing, fingers tapping, hallway chatter—but it all felt distant to Jordan. He kept his eyes on the screen and tried to stay ahead of the subsequent fire. His shoulders ached from hunching forward. He hadn't moved in hours.

The thought came quietly, almost like it belonged to someone else: *Why can't I just push back like Alex does sometimes?*

He didn't say it with bitterness. It wasn't jealousy. It was something closer to resignation.

He remembered that meeting last month—Alex had pushed back on a deadline, calmly but directly. No flinching. Howard had huffed but backed off. Jordan had told himself he couldn't get away with that. But part of him hadn't stopped thinking about it since.

It appeared to Jordan that Alex had boundaries—maybe not perfect ones, but they gave him room to breathe. Jordan had walls. Not the kind that protected, but the kind that boxed him in. They were all inward-facing, built slowly from silence, self-doubt, and unspoken resentment. And lately, they felt like they were getting taller. The room around him was shrinking, the air thinner, the exits harder to find.

He was drowning—but not at work. He was drowning in everything he couldn't stop. Everything he absorbed. Everything he never said.

A deep sigh escaped before he could catch it. His hands hovered over the keyboard.

I'm tired. Not from the work itself, but from never feeling like I could pause without disappointing someone. Especially Howard.

And yet, the longer he played along, the more invisible he felt. His neck felt locked, the muscles pulling tight like cables drawn too far. Even blinking felt like an effort.

He didn't have a solution. No next step. Just the quiet truth pressing against his ribs: He couldn't keep pretending this weight was normal.

And maybe, just maybe—naming the weight was where things started to change.

LEARNING WHERE THE LINE IS

Alex sat with his hands loosely clasped, his gaze drifting toward the window. The late afternoon light cast a soft shadow across the room, and for the first time that day, he looked less restless—tired but present.

"I used to think being dependable meant saying yes," he said. "Even when I didn't agree. Even when it came at a cost."

Carol didn't interrupt. She waited.

"I kept adjusting to Howard's demands," Alex continued. "Every meeting felt like a test, and I convinced myself the best strategy was to stay ahead of him. Predict what he'd want. Fix what he'd criticize before he even noticed. I used to wake up already rehearsing how I'd word things—like if I got the phrasing just right, I could dodge the blow."

He rubbed the side of his face. "I didn't even realize how much time I spent trying not to be wrong." He shook his head. "It worked, I guess. Until it didn't."

Carol nodded. "What changed?"

"I stopped trusting my own judgment. I overanalyzed everything. I second-guessed decisions that were already in motion. And the more I tried to get it right, the more I lost track of what I believed was right." He paused. "I don't know when it started, but it's worn me down."

Carol leaned forward slightly. "It's common in controlling environments for people to take on more than they should. They're not even trying to stand out. They were trying not to be singled out."

Alex nodded in silence. "I think I was so focused on avoiding criticism," he said, "that I stopped noticing when it was crossing a line. Howard even calls me on my day off—about things that don't matter. Stuff that isn't even mine to handle."

Carol raised an eyebrow. "And when that happens, what do you tell yourself?"

Alex looked down. "That it's just easier to respond than deal with the fallout."

Carol nodded slowly. "Do you believe that—deep down?"

He hesitated. "I don't know anymore. Maybe I just got used to it."

She leaned in slightly, voice calm but firm. "Used to what? Being available or being invisible?"

Alex didn't answer right away.

Carol continued, more softly now. "People think boundaries are just about saying no. But it's deeper than that. Boundaries aren't walls—they're signposts. They tell people—and yourself—what's okay and what's not. Without them, you don't disappear all at once. You leak out slowly."

She paused, letting the words settle. "When someone constantly pulls on your time, your energy, your peace—even when it's not urgent, not necessary—and you still say yes out of fear. That's not responsibility. That's erosion."

Alex looked over at her, quieter now.

She added gently, "You don't owe anyone constant accommodation. But you do owe yourself clarity—about what matters, what's yours to carry, and where your line is."

He exhaled slowly. "So, how do you do that?" he asked. "Without shutting people out?"

Carol let the question hang in the air before answering. "Start by naming what's yours—and what's not. Reframe criticism through that lens. Ask yourself, 'Is this feedback helpful, or is it about control?' And when you feel that reflex to over-explain or overcommit, pause. That pause is where the boundary lives."

Alex nodded, thoughtful.

"What would it look like," she asked, "to establish clear boundaries without closing yourself off?"

He didn't respond right away. He finally spoke, voice quiet but clearer. "Maybe it looks like pausing before I say yes. Or asking questions before blindly conceding to what he wants."

Carol nodded once, but said nothing. There was permission in the silence rather than demands.

As the light shifted across the room, Alex felt it again—that faint but steady warmth of clarity as if the sun had moved slightly closer, even if just by an inch.

The Moment of Recoil

The meeting room buzzed with quiet energy, not tense like before but focused. Alex stood at the front, a whiteboard marker in hand, leading a strategy session on a new client integration timeline. Lisa, Jordan, and Mark sat around the table with laptops open, notes scattered, and half-drunk coffees beside them.

Alex had prepared for this. He'd walked into the meeting calm, grounded. He'd even paused outside the door to remind himself of what Carol had said: "You don't have to have all the answers. You just have to lead from what matters to you."

So far, Alex felt things were going well. He was leading with a focus on being relational. The team seemed engaged. Lisa had even smiled once.

"Alright," Alex said, pointing to the projected plan, "This is the rough timeline. We phase in systems access over three weeks and stagger client onboarding alongside compliance."

"If it holds," Mark chimed in, "we can stay ahead of the rollout."

Then, Lisa leaned forward, her voice calm but firm. "I'm not sure this is realistic. Compliance still hasn't finalized approval on the data-sharing protocol. If they push back on access, this whole timeline shifts."

Alex froze inwardly. Something in his chest cinched. His grip on the marker tightened. A flicker of an old reflex lit up inside him. Challenge. Risk. Control slipping. He heard Howard's voice in his head, sharp and scathing: "We don't make excuses. We make it work. Leaders don't hesitate."

Before he could think, the words left his mouth—tight, clipped: "Figure it out." The room went still. Lisa blinked, surprised. Mark looked down. Jordan's eyes drifted toward the window.

It was a small moment. No one said anything. But Alex felt it immediately—the energy shifted. The atmosphere had closed like a door. He'd seen this before. Howard did it all the time. He'd just done it too. Something in him recoiled. He looked at Lisa. She hadn't leaned back, but her posture had changed—guarded now.

Alex took a breath. One second. Two. His breathing helped reset his mind and body.

He dropped the marker onto the tray and turned back to the table. "I'm sorry," he said. His voice was quiet but clear. "That wasn't fair, Lisa."

She looked up, surprised.

"You're right," he continued. "We shouldn't build a plan on assumptions. Let's list out what we're waiting on from compliance. I'll follow up directly this afternoon."

A slight nod from Lisa. Mark raised an eyebrow—impressed, maybe. Jordan, for once, didn't cross his arms. The room reopened. Alex exhaled, his shoulders lowering slightly. Not perfect. But better. He glanced at the whiteboard again, then back at the team.

"Thanks for speaking up," he added. "That's exactly what I need from you."

The tension diffused. Conversations resumed. Lisa started listing dependencies. Mark chimed in with a resource estimate.

Later, at his desk, Alex sat staring at his screen, not reading. The scene replayed in his head—not with shame but curiosity. That was a Howard move, but I caught it. I adjusted. The pause—that had been the turning point.

He opened a new note in his phone and typed a single line: "Slipping up is always a possibility. What matters is seeing when I do."

He saved it and closed the app. Tomorrow, he will try again.

UNLEARNING THE REFLEX

The third session started quietly. There were no dramatic revelations, no weight pressing on the conversation. It was just Alex, sitting a little more comfortably on the couch, arms relaxed at his sides. He was less tired and more present than he had been before.

"I've started paying attention to the moments when I get thrown off," he said. "The times I walk into a meeting and suddenly feel smaller."

Carol leaned forward slightly, her voice low but firm. "And how did it feel, realizing it in the moment?"

Alex let out a breath he hadn't realized he was holding. He rubbed his palms together slowly, thinking."Honestly? At first, it felt like I failed." He glanced down. "That flash of tension—it came out too fast. I didn't even mean to sound like that. It was automatic."

He paused, then looked up again. "But then, I caught it. I saw the reaction in the room—how Lisa pulled back, how the team shut down. And I heard myself. It was like I was watching the old me show up, the one who just wanted to avoid making waves, to stay in control."

Carol nodded gently, staying with him. "And what did you do with that awareness?"

"I stopped," Alex said. "I paused. And I changed course. I owned it. I apologized and asked a better question." He shrugged. "It wasn't perfect. But it felt different. Like I had room to choose something else."

Carol gave a faint, satisfied smile. "That's self-leadership, Alex. Not just knowing what went wrong, but noticing the moment you could choose again. Most people only reflect after the damage is done. But you noticed it in real time."

Alex absorbed that, sitting with the weight and truth of it. "It was just a second. But it mattered." He leaned back. "For once, I didn't need to be right. I just needed to be real. That pause gave me that."

Carol smiled again, this time more fully. "That pause is the space between reaction and intention. That's where leaders are made."

Alex gave a small smile and nodded slowly. He felt that the statement was something he could carry forward.

Chapter 6

Jordan's Quiet Realization

The meeting had ended an hour ago, but its weight lingered. Jordan sat alone at his desk, the usual post-meeting shuffle absent. There were no casual follow-ups, no side conversations, just silence thick enough to notice.

He clicked through a few tabs on his screen, pretending to focus, but his thoughts stayed locked on how things unfolded. Alex had been out, but it had been enough to throw the team off. Questions came faster than answers, and Jordan had stepped in to keep things moving.

Except he hadn't kept things moving. He'd snapped. He could still see how Lisa's expression shifted when he cut her off mid-sentence. Mark stopped volunteering ideas after Jordan dismissed his suggestion with a flat "That won't work." It hadn't been intentional. But it had been sharp. Too sharp.

As the office settled into a lull, Jordan felt it in his chest—a slow burn of guilt, heavy and familiar. He sat back in his chair and let his eyes wander across the floor. No one had said anything directly. But they didn't have to. He could feel the shift. The team was tense. And it started with him.

"I'm acting just like Howard," he thought. The words came without resistance. "Impatient. Critical. Distant."

But this time, the thought of it stung and stuck. Something else surfaced uninvited. A memory from a few months ago came to mind.

They'd just wrapped up a team review, and Howard had been in full force—methodical, emotionless, gutting people with surgical precision. One teammate, Erin, had fumbled a presentation slide, and Howard used it as an opportunity to undermine her entirely.

"If this is your version of excellence, we've got bigger problems than this timeline."

The room had gone silent. Jordan hadn't said anything. No one had. They'd just looked down and tried not to be next.

But afterward, he remembered this clearly—Alex had pulled Erin aside in the hallway. Jordan had lingered nearby, pretending to check his phone. He heard just enough.

"You're not the problem," Alex had told her. "That pressure back there—that wasn't about your slide. It was about control. You've been doing solid work. Let's talk through how to pivot and avoid panic."

Jordan remembered how Erin's shoulders dropped—just an inch—but enough to see she'd been carrying more than the task. He hadn't thought much of it then. He was just relieved it hadn't been him.

But now, as he sat there thinking back on the tension in that meeting, he realized he'd done the opposite. He was the one who had dismissed others—the one whom people braced themselves for.

"I'm turning into the leader I once needed protection from."

He sat back in his chair, eyes burning slightly. He didn't know when the line had blurred. But now he saw it. Clearly.

He was tired and stopped showing up as he once believed a good leader should. He'd been mimicking safety by enforcing control—a mask that looked like leadership but felt like fear.

Jordan closed his laptop slowly. There was nothing to finish in this state. "Maybe I need to start where Alex did," he thought. "With honesty. Even if it's messy."

He stood up, his chair squeaking behind him, and walked to the breakroom to breathe. To make space. For the first time in a long time, he wasn't afraid of the discomfort.

He poured himself a cup of coffee and pulled out his phone to check for unread emails. An internal email floated through the inbox a few days ago.

EMAIL **a few days ago**

Strategy Alignment Q4: Leadership Sync

It was vague and noticeable. Usually, that meant org chart updates were on the way.

Going the New Way Forward

The hour had passed quickly, though neither of them had been watching the clock. Carol sat with her notebook on her knee, open but still mostly blank. She hadn't needed to write much. Alex had done most of the work himself.

She leaned forward slightly. "Before we wrap up, I want to offer a few small steps—just to keep the ground you've gained today."

Alex nodded. "I'm listening."

"Nothing complicated," she said. "Start with boundaries. In conversation, in meetings—pause before you say yes. Give yourself space to think. You don't have to take on everything just because it's handed to you."

He gave a quiet laugh. "That one might take practice."

"That's the point," she said with a smile. "And give credit where it's due. When your team shows up—acknowledge it. Even small affirmations can go a long way in shifting the atmosphere."

Alex nodded again, slower this time.

"And at the end of each day, take a few minutes to reflect," she continued. "Don't focus on what went wrong, but on what aligned. What felt right—what felt like you."

"Journaling?" he asked.

"Could be," she said. "Or just a mental check-in. One win a day. Even if it's small."

He thought back to that meeting, when Lisa relaxed and Jordan nodded in agreement. Maybe that was a win. That could be a good starting point.

"I think I've spent a lot of time focusing on what I'm doing wrong," he said. "Trying to avoid slipping up again."

Carol nodded. "That's common when feedback has been tied to fear. But the goal here isn't perfection but becoming whole."

Alex looked over at her, his gaze lifted as he considered it. "I can do that. Or—I want to work toward it."

Alex wasn't sure when those words became something he meant, but he did. Not perfectly. Not yet. But the gap between knowing and doing didn't feel impossible anymore.

She smiled. "Then start there. Build trust with your team. Trust yourself a little more each day. And when fear starts creeping in, just notice it. You don't have to act on it."

He took a breath, steady and slow. "I know I'll slip up. Old habits are stubborn."

"They are," Carol agreed. "But you've already started noticing them. That's the difference."

Alex leaned forward slightly, elbows on his knees. "I'll keep going. Even if it's slow."

Carol nodded. "Don't worry about that. Growth isn't linear. But awareness is movement. And that movement matters."

He stood, brushing his hands against the side of his jeans, then looked at Carol and offered his hand. She took it without hesitation—firm, steady, no formality.

Alex held her gaze for a moment, then gave a slight nod. "Thank you for all your help."

Their hands dropped, and the silence that followed wasn't empty—he had earned it. Alex didn't have every answer, but he was leaving with something better: permission to lead as himself.

Alex exited the therapy room, the load on his shoulders considerably lighter.

Chapter 6

Jordan Watches the Shift

There was a stillness in the air—the kind that came before a shift. Something beneath the surface had started to realign, and Jordan could feel it before he could name it.

Jordan leaned against the doorway to the breakroom, coffee cooling in his hand as he watched Alex across the bullpen. Alex was with the team, listening as Lisa addressed a client's concern. His posture was open, his expression steady. He wasn't rushing to solve or prove he had the correct answer. He just listened—really listened—and asked for a follow-up that showed he understood.

The group's tone had softened—not casual, but less tense, focused, and collaborative. And Alex, for all his recent wear and tear, looked clearer.

Jordan took a sip of his coffee and kept watching. He'd seen Alex struggle. Seen the weight on his shoulders, the second-guessing, the hesitation. But now, something about how he moved through conversations—the patience and the calm—looked less like survival and more like direction.

He remembered that Alex had pulled Lisa aside a week ago after Howard snapped in the morning meeting. Not to correct her, not to scold—just to check in. At the time, Jordan had dismissed it as soft. Now? He wasn't so sure it hadn't been courage.

Jordan turned back toward his desk, and the hallway was quiet around him. Sitting down, he felt a dull discomfort settle in his chest. It was not envy, not judgment, just the slow realization that he couldn't remember the last time he'd felt growth in his leadership. It felt heavier than that. Maybe regret. Or the quiet weight of realizing he'd stopped expecting more from his team, from himself.

He'd gotten good at getting through the day. Good at staying out of trouble, keeping pace, and avoiding the spotlight. He'd chalked it up to staying focused. Keeping things smooth.

But lately, that invisibility had come with a cost. The team no longer sought guidance from Jordan—they had stopped expecting it. Somewhere along the way, Jordan had become easy to overlook. And maybe that was the point.

But watching Alex now, after everything, Jordan wasn't so sure that smooth was the same thing as steady. He wondered, *Have I just been avoiding friction? Avoiding risk?*

He stared at his screen, then let his gaze drift back toward the team. Alex stood beside Mark, calmly walking him through a planning document. There was no grand speech, no performance, just presence.

Jordan exhaled through his nose. *Maybe I've been hiding behind comfort.* The thought didn't feel dramatic. It felt overdue.

Jordan stayed quiet as the afternoon rolled forward, watching Alex from across the room. And he didn't look away when the discomfort crept in for the first time. He stayed with it.

Maybe it's time I figured out who I am as a leader, too—even if it means stepping out of the version of myself that's kept me safe.

UNEXPECTED DEVELOPMENT

Just as Jordan turned back to his screen, an alert popped up in the corner—an all-staff email from executive leadership. The subject line was short, but it caught his eye immediately.

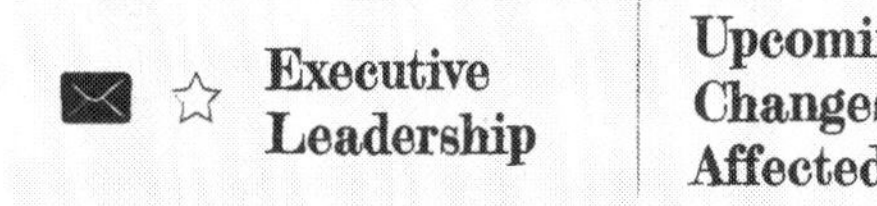

He opened it, skimming the message.

The company had entered into a "strategic merger agreement" with a competitor. No names. No hierarchy. Just polished ambiguity. It was still early, but changes were already underway—structural ones, leadership shifts, and team realignments. But between the lines, it was clear: A merger was in motion.

Jordan read it twice, then leaned back in his chair. Across the office, Alex was still with the team, unaware. Jordan's stomach tightened—not with panic, but with the weight of uncertainty. Everything that had felt fragile now hung in the air again.

He looked at the email one last time, then closed it without saying a word.

Reflect

1. When was the last time you felt like you were "shrinking" instead of showing up as your full self?
2. When do you feel most disconnected from your values in a leadership role? What triggers that disconnection?
3. What does healthy leadership look like to you, and how does it feel different from fear-based leadership you've experienced or witnessed?
4. Are there moments when you've led from instinct but second-guessed yourself afterward? What might it take to start trusting those instincts again?
5. Where do you see signs of internalized criticism showing up in your daily life or leadership habits?
6. Think about someone who models grounded, values-driven leadership. What do they do differently—and what can you learn from them?

Action

1. Identify one small boundary you can set this week—whether in a meeting, an email, or a conversation—that protects your focus or energy.

2. Practice pausing before responding in a high-pressure moment. What shifts when you give yourself even five seconds to breathe?
3. At the end of the day, jot down one moment where you led in a way that aligned with your values. Do this daily for the next week.
4. Choose one teammate to affirm genuinely this week, not for performance, but for presence, contribution, or character.
5. When fear shows up in your leadership, how will you name it rather than react to it? Write down one question you'll use to check in with yourself.
6. What's one way you can lead from authenticity tomorrow—whether that means being transparent, asking for help, or listening more intentionally?

Dear Alex,

Do the hard work.

-Casey

CHAPTER 7

The Turning Point

Leadership in Action

The greatest danger in times of turbulence is not the turbulence—it's to act with yesterday's logic."

-Peter Drucker

The office didn't feel like itself. Phones rang endlessly, unanswered. Desks once humming with familiar rhythms now buzzed with fragmented energy. A manager's voice cracked across the room, sharp and rushed, trying to untangle yet another reporting mix-up. Just beyond the bullpen, near the client service desk, a tense exchange was unfolding.

"I already sent the proposal file—check your inbox," said Nadia, a Horizon Valley rep, her voice clipped.

"I'm telling you, I sent it yesterday," countered Theo, a newly assigned Summitpoint Solutions account manager. "You duplicated the outreach. The client just called—confused and annoyed."

Nadia turned, eyes wide. "Because no one told me you were handling it. You weren't even in the loop last week."

Theo held up his tablet, flashing the sent timestamp. "Well, I am now."

Their voices rose, not angry but tight with urgency, just loud enough to draw glances from nearby desks. A junior sales analyst nearby hesitated mid-keystroke, clearly listening. Across the aisle, Lisa looked up from her monitor, brows pinched.

Alex stepped into this fraying edge of the floor just as the standoff was peaking. He didn't need to hear the whole exchange—he saw the client's name on the whiteboard, underlined and circled twice. It was their largest contract.

He scanned the room. Summitpoint badges dotted the bullpen like misplaced puzzle pieces, team leads standing awkwardly behind desks they didn't recognize, conversations halting mid-sentence as people tried to figure out who was still "in charge."

The moment revealed fractured communication and a loss of trust.

He caught sight of Lisa, frozen at her desk. Jordan hovered a few feet away, his jaw tight.

"We just got the email," Lisa said, voice hollow. "Our biggest client—done."

Alex moved closer, his voice calm and steady. "Define 'done.'"

"They're already exploring competitors," she said, slowly facing him. "With the Summitpoint merger happening, they don't see stability or a future here."

Jordan leaned back, letting out a low, bitter breath. "Perfect timing. Maybe we should wait for Howard. He always has insight."

Alex glanced at him but didn't respond. Howard was off-site, finalizing the details of the new Horizon Valley after the merger, locked in an executive room somewhere. His absence was palpable. The team dealt with the client fallout while they were leaderless and unmoored.

Alex hesitated for a breath, just long enough to feel the weight of it all—the merger, the client, the silence. Then, something in him clicked. "Everyone," he said, steady and clear, "Conference room. Five minutes."

No one argued. The team just moved.

ALEX TAKES THE LEAD

The conference room was half-lit by a row of windows overlooking the street, but no one took notice of the view. The table was cluttered—pages of meeting notes, unopened Summitpoint protocol manuals, and hastily printed client data littered the surface. An untouched stack of binders sat near the wall, one teetering too close to the edge, like a visual metaphor no one had the energy to acknowledge.

Outside the glass doors, raised voices clashed in the hallway. A Summitpoint supervisor argued with a Horizon Valley manager about who was responsible for handling a shared client portfolio. No one in the room flinched. By now, they had gotten used to it.

Alex stood at the head of the table, every pair of eyes turned toward him, but it felt different than before. It wasn't just pressure. It was permission. Still, his grip on the back of the chair tightened for a second longer than it needed to.

He glanced at Lisa, then Jordan. The papers were in disarray across the table.

"I think we should consider waiting," he started, voice quieter than intended. "Maybe Howard can—"

He stopped mid-sentence, catching the slight narrowing of Lisa's eyes. Jordan shifted back in his seat, folding his arms again. The hesitation sat there, loud and unwelcome.

Alex felt it. That old reflex—to defer, to wait for someone else's call. No. He drew a breath, straightened his shoulders, and reset.

"No," he said, firmer now. "We've waited long enough. Our biggest client is looking elsewhere, and if we don't act, we lose them. We either step up or let this place unravel."

A quiet pause followed—not tense, but alert. Lisa's posture softened. Jordan unfolded his arms, just slightly.

Alex met their eyes again, steadier this time. "Here's what we do. First, Lisa, get the client on the phone."

No one said anything at first—just a few silent nods and a shift in posture. The tension didn't vanish, but it paused—like the room had exhaled together without meaning to.

Jordan looked back at Alex. He didn't speak again, but his expression had changed—it was less guarded and more watchful. Something was happening, and Jordan was ready to embrace it.

The Balcony Moment

The rooftop balcony gave just enough distance to breathe. Alex stood alone, leaning on the railing, eyes fixed on the skyline but focused elsewhere. Below, the city moved at its own pace, unbothered by mergers or missed emails. There was something steady about it, even as everything in his world felt like it was shifting underfoot.

From where he stood, Alex could see unfamiliar Summitpoint Solutions employees filtering through the courtyard—clipboards in hand, badges bouncing on lanyards, eyes scanning a building that still didn't feel like theirs. Horizon Valley didn't feel quite like his, either.

He rubbed a thumb along the railing's edge. The team had followed his lead that morning. Lisa stepped up without hesitation. Jordan had stayed engaged, watching closely. They were trying to find direction, and for a moment, they looked to him. That meant something. But now, in the stillness, the doubt returned.

What if I just got lucky?

The door behind him clicked open. Casey stepped out, coffee in hand, her pace unrushed. She stood next to him without speaking, letting the quiet stretch comfortably between them. She didn't fill the silence—she matched it.

I heard about your promotion," Alex said after a moment. "VP of Marketing—congratulations."

"Thank you." Casey smiled.

Alex exhaled, still looking out at the skyline. "Feels like the ground keeps moving."

Casey nodded, sipping. "It is. Everyone's waiting for the dust to settle, but I don't think it will anytime soon."

He gave a half-smile. "Not exactly the most comforting thing I've heard today."

"Didn't say it to scare you," she replied. "It's just where we are. Mergers always stir up uncertainty, especially when no one knows who's staying in what seat."

Alex nodded again, slower this time. "There's so much noise. Everyone wants answers, and I barely have any for myself."

Casey tilted her head. "You had enough clarity to lead the team, though."

"I didn't even think about leadership," Alex admitted. "I just knew someone had to step in."

"Exactly," she said. "You saw the gap. You filled it. That's leadership."

He was quiet for a moment. "I keep hoping someone will step in and say, 'You've got this. Keep going.'" He shrugged. "But no one does."

She looked out toward the skyline again. "They won't. Not in a merger. Not in a company stuck in transition. That kind of clarity has to come from you."

Alex turned to look at her, eyes searching. "How do you know when you're doing it right?"

She smiled softly. "You know when you're doing it in alignment with who you are. You can only focus on maturing yourself in the process. Being patient and kind with others."

He looked down at the courtyard—people walking, shifting, wondering where they belonged.

"I keep waiting for the green light," he said. "For some sign that it's okay to trust my instincts."

Casey rested her cup on the railing. "You don't need a green light. Stability doesn't come from waiting—it comes from leading, even when things are still messy."

Alex didn't say anything right away. But the silence that followed felt different. Not empty—just open.

He nodded, the tension in his posture softening. His shoulders didn't lighten completely, but they no longer held the weight of trying to prove something. It wasn't about having a title or the whole picture. It was about showing up—on the balcony, in the boardroom, and in the moments that mattered.

It was about starting here.

48 HOURS

The glass conference room had always carried a certain weight, primarily hosting high-stakes client meetings, where teams made real-time decisions. Today, that weight felt heavier than usual.

Lisa and Jordan sat across from Alex, each with a thick binder open in front of them. One was labeled "Horizon Valley: Client Management Protocols," and the other "Summitpoint Solutions: Client Interaction Guidelines." Tabs and highlights marked both, but neither offered absolute clarity. Lisa scanned the pages one last time while Jordan flipped between conflicting sections, muttering under his breath.

Alex sat with the speakerphone in front of him, postured upright, his hands steady. The phone rang twice. Then, the client picked up—his voice sharp, tension immediate.

"We've had enough," the client snapped. "We don't even know who we're dealing with anymore—Horizon Valley or Summitpoint Solutions. We're going to explore other options."

Alex answered in a steady voice. "I completely understand the confusion," he said, calm but direct. "Right now, let's focus on how we can fix this—starting today."

The client answered him with a long pause before speaking again. "Honestly," the client said, voice still clipped, "we're already looking at other vendors."

Alex leaned slightly forward, voice clear and composed. "Give us 48 hours. Let us clarify exactly how this merger benefits you. If after that you still aren't convinced we're your best option, I'll personally make sure the transition is painless."

Another pause, but longer this time. Just the faint hum of the line. Then, a reluctant sigh. "Fine—48 hours."

Alex nodded, even though the client couldn't see it. "Thank you. We'll be in touch well before then."

He ended the call gently, not slamming the button or slumping back—just a quiet, deliberate press of the keypad. The silence that followed in the room was different—less tense and more stunned.

Lisa whispered, "So, we bought ourselves some time."

Alex didn't smile. He didn't let himself relax. "Yeah," he said. "Now, let's make it count."

Jordan flipped one of the binders closed with more force than necessary. "For what it's worth," he muttered, "these protocol binders contradict each other on practically every point. Neither one helped much."

Lisa glanced down at her notes, then back up at Alex—not just hearing his words, but watching him. His expression was composed, but she could tell he was holding the weight for all of them.

For months, she'd watched him hesitate, wait for permission, and second-guess decisions. Today was different. The call had been clear. The tone had been calm. And when the client pushed back, Alex hadn't deflected—he'd stepped in.

She felt something shift. Not just trust but relief like someone had finally picked up the weight she hadn't realized she'd been carrying.

Quietly, almost too softly to hear, she murmured, "You're becoming the kind of leader this place actually needs."

Alex didn't respond. Maybe he hadn't heard it, or he didn't need to. But she meant it.

INITIATIVE OR INSUBORDINATION?

A hush swept over the bullpen, silencing clicks, chatter, and half-finished conversations. The glass door opened. Howard entered.

He didn't speak. He didn't need to. Dressed in sharp, charcoal gray, he moved as if he owned the space.

Across the floor, posture shifted. A junior analyst dropped a file, papers skidding in all directions. Lisa's fingers froze mid-keystroke. Jordan straightened. Even the Summitpoint reps sensed it—an unspoken shift, like a cold draft you couldn't trace.

Howard's eyes swept the room like a silent audit. No nod. No scowl. Just presence.

Then, without a word, he turned and disappeared into his office. The glass door clicked shut.

Alex watched from across the floor as Howard calmly scanned a report, flipping pages as if gathering data—and leverage. His pace was quiet. Precise. But every movement said the same thing: *"I'm still watching."*

"Alex. Come in," he said, calm and neutral.

Inside Howard's office, light filtered through half-closed blinds, striping the floor and casting uneven shadows across the table. A neatly organized stack of folders sat on one side of the desk, each labeled with transition plans, sales updates, and merger notes. The topmost read "VP of Sales Transition Brief – Howard."

Alex stepped in and closed the door behind him. He stood for a moment before Howard gestured for him to sit. Neither rushed the moment nor did they fill it with unnecessary small talk.

"I heard you took the lead earlier," Howard said finally, voice even.

Alex nodded once. "The situation called for action."

Howard leaned back slightly in his chair, elbows resting on the armrests, hands folded loosely. "And you believe you handled it well?"

"We bought time with the client—48 hours to keep the relationship intact," Alex said. "It gave us a window to stabilize things."

There was no reaction from Howard, and no indication of agreement or disapproval was evident. He studied Alex carefully before speaking again. "And you made that call without running it through me."

"You weren't reachable," Alex said, keeping his tone even.

"True," Howard replied, smoothing the cuff of his sleeve. "And you'll find that'll be the case more often now—my new role demands that I operate at a higher altitude."

He let the moment hang, his gaze lingering just long enough to make it uncomfortable.

"Which makes it even more important that people on the ground know their place," he added, his tone calm, almost instructional. "It raises the real question: When does initiative become disobedience masked as leadership?"

The room grew still and heavy with a quiet, more calculated presence. Howard's words didn't come with heat but with something colder—curiosity, perhaps. Or a test disguised as casual reflection.

Alex didn't immediately respond. He recognized the silence for what it was: Deliberate space meant to invite doubt. But he kept his posture steady, his hands still.

Howard reached for a pen, turning it slowly between his fingers as he looked across the desk. "You did what you thought was best," he said finally, the words shaped with calm distance. "Let's see if it was."

"We'll have results within the deadline," Alex replied, keeping his tone just above neutral.

Howard offered the faintest tilt of his head, somewhere between a nod and a challenge. He set the pen down and leaned back slightly in his chair. "You're aware, of course, that I've officially accepted the VP of Sales position."

Alex held still, absorbing the news. "I'd heard it was in motion."

Howard smirked, barely. "It's more than motion now. And with that move comes a vacancy—my current role."

He let the pause stretch just long enough.

"There's interest from both sides—Horizon Valley and Summitpoint Solutions. I've seen a shortlist. Your name's on it," he said, tapping the corner of the folder with two fingers. "So is Lisa's. Jordan's. And two Summitpoint department heads. They're watching closely. So am I."

The words weren't congratulations. They were bait—the kind Howard preferred—designed to raise hopes just enough to leave room for self-doubt.

Alex met his gaze. "Understood."

Howard offered a measured smile, the kind that never quite reached his eyes. "Leadership in transition is delicate. You handled the client call. Now, we'll see if that was leadership—or luck."

Alex's jaw tightened, but he kept his voice even. "I believe in the team's work. We'll let the results speak."

Howard leaned forward, resting his arms on the desk. "Just remember—being under consideration isn't the same as being ready."

There was no formal dismissal, just the subtle shift of Howard's attention back to the papers in front of him. The conversation was over.

Alex stood and turned toward the door. He was unclear whether Howard had acknowledged or undermined him, but one thing was sure: Everyone was watching him, not just Howard.

THE LEADERSHIP LIMBO

The café inside Horizon Valley had once been a place of easy rhythm—soft jazz in the background, the occasional hiss of the espresso machine, conversations rising and falling without tension. Now, the scent of freshly brewed coffee couldn't settle the unease. Employees from both companies sat at scattered tables, heads bowed over laptops and merger binders, voices lowered but still carrying the same unresolved tone.

At a nearby counter, two project managers, one from Summitpoint and one from Horizon, stood shoulder to shoulder, locked in a polite but circular debate about overlapping reporting structures.

Alex sat at a window table, his coffee untouched for too long. The spoon still rested in the mug, but he'd stopped stirring it minutes ago. His focus wasn't on the crowded café or the movement outside the glass. His thoughts were stuck on Howard—his words, tone, and most of all, how he'd left the room without giving anything away. It wasn't outright disapproval, but neither was it approval. The middle space between the two had left Alex suspended.

Across from him, Casey slid into the seat with practiced ease, a fresh cup of coffee in hand. She glanced around, taking in the tension that hung in the air like steam, before settling her eyes on him.

"So," she said, studying his face carefully, "how did it go with Howard?"

Alex exhaled, his hand drifting to the edge of his cup but not lifting it. "I don't know. He didn't yell or get mad. He just... assessed."

Casey nodded, not surprised. " He doesn't need to. That's not how he leads."

Alex gave a tired nod of agreement. "Yeah. He framed it as a question—'When does initiative become disobedience masked as leadership?'"

As she sipped from her cup, her expression remained thoughtful. "And what do you think?"

He paused before answering. "I think I did what had to be done."

Her smile was faint, almost imperceptible, but it was there. "Then why do you still look like you're waiting for the other shoe to drop?"

Alex leaned back, shifting his weight in the chair as he ran a hand through his hair. He let his breath come slower this time, recalling what Carol had told him just days earlier—to focus on the present moment. Don't let someone else's silence turn into your own story. Still, it was easier said than done.

"I don't know what he's thinking," he said. "He didn't tell me I did well, but he didn't tell me I screwed up either."

"He won't," Casey replied, setting her cup down gently. "That's the strategy of Howard's leadership. He always makes sure you don't know where you stand."

Alex looked down at the table, his fingers brushing the edge of a napkin. "So, what am I supposed to do? Play it safe?"

"No," she said firmly. "Keep leading. Keep making decisions."

He looked up again. "Even if he's waiting for me to fail?"

She shrugged slightly. "Especially then."

Casey paused for a bit before she continued. "Howard's model has worked for a long time. He knows how to hold control without having to raise his voice. But this place isn't what it used to be. People are asking different questions now. Expectations are shifting. If you're waiting for him to validate what you're doing, you'll be stuck in limbo."

"So, I'm on my own," Alex said, quieter this time, more reflection than complaint.

She shook her head gently. "No. You have your team. And from what I've seen, they're starting to believe in you."

The statement didn't land like a compliment. It felt steadier than that—like an observation rooted in truth. Alex glanced around the café, taking in the faces of coworkers who had followed him into a shaky client meeting, who hadn't argued when he called them together. The people around him weren't waiting for Howard anymore. They were waiting for clarity, and for the first time, they were looking to him to provide it.

He turned back to Casey, his voice new and resolved. "We have 48 hours to fix this."

With a faint smile, she raised her coffee cup. "Then here's a toast to you."

Alex picked up his cup and met her toast, the edges of doubt giving way—if not to full confidence, then at least to forward motion.

A STONE IN THE WATER

Jordan sat two tables behind Alex and Casey, half-shielded by a tall potted plant and the slow churn of café noise that made eavesdropping less intentional and more inevitable. He hadn't meant to overhear the entire conversation. But once it started, he couldn't stop listening.

His coffee had long since cooled. He held the mug loosely between his hands, turning it just enough to feel the ceramic shift beneath his fingers. Around him, the usual undercurrent of quiet merger talk hummed—strained voices sorting out overlapping responsibilities, just loud enough to register but not enough to interrupt his thoughts.

The past few hours played out in his mind with quiet precision. Alex had called the emergency meeting. He assigned roles, took the client's call, and stood firm in front of a room full of uncertainty. Somehow, he made the team believe they weren't unraveling. Howard, meanwhile, had been off-site, preoccupied with transition strategy, and unavailable when the pressure had peaked. And despite that, or maybe because of it, the team had held together.

His gaze drifted toward Alex, then dropped to the table. He remembered something from months ago—something small, but it had stuck.

It was late. Jordan sifted through a metrics report full of mismatched data, the deadline pressing in around him. Howard had hovered behind him for nearly ten minutes, offering no help, just questions that sounded more like traps.

After Howard left, Alex had walked by, glanced at Jordan's screen, and paused.

"Hey," Alex had said quietly. "I've been there."

Jordan had braced for a critique, but instead, Alex pulled up a chair. For the next 20 minutes, he helped untangle the mess—without judgment, without claiming credit, without reporting it upward. He simply showed up and helped.

Jordan stared into his mug now, the memory pressing into the moment. That was leadership, he thought. I just didn't see it then.

Back at their table, Alex and Casey had gone quiet. Alex leaned in slightly, posture steady, eyes clear. There was no performance for him. No show. Just presence. Jordan hadn't always appreciated that, but now, he was starting to.

Alex may deserve the promotion, he thought. Not because he's loud or flawless, but because he shows up when it matters.

The idea landed like a stone in water, rippling outward, undeniable. Jordan didn't know what to do with it yet, but something in him had already shifted.

THE CLIENT MEETING

Forty-eight hours after the call, Alex didn't return to the glass conference room. Instead, he caught a ride across town and sat face-to-face with Michael, the client whose account had once anchored Horizon Valley's portfolio.

They met in a quiet office, the kind with leather chairs and an abundance of calendars. Michael wasn't angry—just tired. Disappointed. Ready to walk.

Alex didn't bring slides. No printed proposal. Just a notepad and the confidence that came from doing the work.

"We identified where we dropped the ball—mainly communication," Alex said plainly. "Too many points of contact. Not enough clarity. The merger made a mess of things."

Michael gave a slow nod but said nothing. He folded his arms across his chest.

"But," Alex continued, "what matters more than any process is our relationship with you. I know the uncertainty is frustrating, and I understand if you need to go in another direction. But if you're willing, I'll take full ownership of this account personally. I'll make sure you have one point of contact—and real follow-through."

Michael's gaze didn't soften right away, but it settled. "You're not here to save face," he said finally. "You're here because you care about us?"

"I do," Alex said.

Michael leaned back. "Then that matters more than any process. You've got the business. Just send over the revised terms."

Alex stood and shook his hand firmly—no pretense. "Thank you, Michael."

As soon as he stepped outside, he dialed Lisa and Jordan.

"We got them back," he said, unable to keep the note of quiet relief from his voice.

Jordan let out a low whistle. Lisa didn't say anything at first, just an audible breath on the other end. Then: "You pulled it off."

"No—we did," Alex replied. "I'll be back soon.

When Alex returned to Horizon Valley, the energy was different—subtle, the kind of shift you notice only when the noise finally stops.

As he passed the bullpen, heads lifted—not in fanfare, but in acknowledgment. Lisa looked up first, then gave a slow, confident nod. Jordan didn't say anything, but the corner of his mouth turned slightly. The team didn't need a debrief. The trust was already there.

He kept walking, heart still settling. Then came Howard. The corridor was quiet. Howard stood with his arms folded, his posture as unreadable as always. He'd been waiting.

"Nice recovery," Howard said. The words were measured, offered with the faintest trace of something between acknowledgment and distance.

Alex didn't break stride. "The team deserves the credit. They pulled together quickly."

Howard gave a small, tight, ambiguous smile. "Securing an extended contract—that's a big win. Just remember, consistency is harder than crisis management. Especially now."

Alex watched Howard walk away, the sharp lines of his tailored suit retreating into the turn of the hallway, shoulders rigid, pace unhurried. No congratulations. No final word. Just distance, as always.

But this time, Alex didn't follow with his thoughts. Instead, he turned back toward the conference room.

The door was ajar now, still humming with the low sounds of quiet debrief—rustling papers, a low laugh, someone exhaling with relief. Through the glass, Alex could see Lisa flipping through the client packet one last time. Jordan leaned slightly toward her, murmuring something that made her smirk. The tension from two days ago had thinned, replaced not with celebration, but something steadier. Composure. Trust.

As Alex approached, people regarded him with subtle shifts in posture, a few straightening their backs, and quiet glances that acknowledged his presence, not as Howard's proxy, but as their leader.

Alex stood a moment longer before stepping back into the room, his mind filled with clarity. He didn't need to prove himself anymore. He just needed to keep showing up—aligned, grounded, and leading forward.

As he crossed the threshold, a quiet thought surfaced—steady, simple, and true: *Leadership starts when you return to what grounds you.*

And for the first time in a long while, Alex knew what that meant.

REFLECT

1. When have you experienced a shift in leadership—either stepping up yourself or watching someone else do it? What did that moment reveal about your team's dynamics?

2. How does fear of judgment influence the way you lead? When was the last time you allowed uncertainty to shape your decisions?

3. What does it feel like when leadership becomes more about presence than control? Have you ever confused urgency with panic in your leadership? How did that play out?

4. Howard's ambiguity left Alex in a constant state of uncertainty. How do unclear power dynamics affect your confidence and decision-making?

5. Jordan began to question the leadership model he had long respected. What does "leading from alignment" mean to you personally?

6. Casey told Alex, "If you wait for Howard to validate your actions, you'll stay stuck in limbo." Who are you still waiting for validation from, and what would it mean to move forward without it?

ACTION

1. How is your team doing? Schedule a 15-minute check-in with your team this week. Don't give directions—just listen.

2. Reframe a mistake you made recently as a moment of leadership in motion. What did you learn?

3. Take five minutes to reflect on a recent leadership moment. Did you lead with control, or did you create stability? What would you do differently next time?
4. How would you respond if a team member were to step into a leadership role unexpectedly? What can you do now to prepare others for that possibility?
5. This week, find one opportunity to affirm someone's leadership instincts—especially if they're still learning to trust themselves.

To Alex,

If you're waiting for him to validate what you're doing, you'll be stuck in limbo.

– From Casey

CHAPTER 8

Building Collaborative Teams

The strength of the team is each individual member. The strength of each member is the team."

-Phil Jackson

The office floor buzzed with a different energy—it felt low-level and restless. It was heavier than deadlines or meetings, something more challenging to put into words.

Horizon Valley and Summitpoint Solutions employees now shared rows of desks and software, but didn't share rhythm. Not yet. People clipped conversations short. Eye contact came cautiously, if at all.

A Summitpoint team lead challenged a workflow at full volume across the aisle, and Mark, seated nearby, winced as if the sound itself scraped.

Two Summitpoint analysts working with Alex and the team, Alicia and Brent, sat side by side near the middle of the floor, physically present and professionally guarded.

Alicia scrolled through an unfamiliar dashboard with surgical focus, clicking with a speed that dared interruption. Brent leaned back in his chair, headphones around his neck, eyes half-fixed on his screen, half on the Horizon Valley team, threading a quiet conversation across the room.

They weren't disruptive, but they weren't aligned. It wasn't open resistance. It was something more subtle. Withholding. Skeptical. Observant. Waiting to see who would stumble first.

Alex stood inside his new office—the one that used to be Howard's. Strange how quickly the physical space had changed and how slowly the feeling of it caught up.

He set a small plant down near the window, something he'd grabbed from his apartment that morning, and adjusted a stack of folders without looking at them too closely.

He was trying not to think about how many times he had sat in this same room before, back straight, every word measured, never sure if he belonged.

Now, the office was his. Someone had already updated the nameplate on the door. The bookshelves were less curated, and the whiteboard was half full of diagrams no one had bothered to erase. The room smelled faintly of fresh paint—and beneath it, something else. Something like expectation.

A single dark gray pen sat at the center of the desk, just above a clean legal pad. Tucked under it was a small note in Casey's handwriting:

> For someone who finally stopped asking for permission. Never let anyone dismiss your strengths. And never dismiss anyone else's strengths.

He didn't say anything when he read it—just let a quiet smile pull at the corner of his mouth. Of course, Casey would leave something like that. Professional. Pointed. Encouraging in a way no one needed to explain. He tucked the note into a drawer to keep it close.

He sat down and pulled the top report off the stack. Some were from Lisa, others from Summitpoint Solutions. The data lacked coherence. One system reported in metrics, the other in milestones. Horizon tracks by department, and Summitpoint by function. It was less like merging two companies and more like trying to translate a language mid-conversation.

There was a knock on the glass—soft but brisk. Lisa and Jordan stepped in together. Lisa handed him a printed update, her expression tired but sharp.

"Mark just flagged a systems mismatch on the reporting end," she said flatly. "Looks like Summitpoint's workflow overrides ours."

Alex skimmed the page. "Are we losing data?"

"No," she replied, "just time. Everything's double-entry right now. It's slow, and everyone's frustrated."

He leaned back in the chair and let the paper fall to the desk. "Alright. Let's stop putting people where they land and start putting them where they lead. I'll handle Summitpoint. You start mapping tasks to actual strengths."

Lisa nodded, already thinking it through as she turned to leave.

Jordan stayed a step behind, quiet. He said nothing, but his eyes remained on Alex longer than usual. There wasn't any skepticism—not this time. If anything, there was a shift in posture, a stillness that didn't look like resistance. Maybe it was curiosity. Maybe something closer to respect.

Alex didn't comment. He just returned to the desk, scanning the next set of numbers. He knew what this role could turn into if he let it. It wasn't about being the person who replaced Howard, but refusing to lead the way Howard had. The real work was about creating space for others to do their best work, even the ones who didn't trust him yet.

This office used to intimidate people, he thought. I need it to do the opposite. If I try to do this alone, we will fail. We must play to our strengths—or we won't stand a chance.

A FIRE INSIDE OR CAUSING FIRES

The rooftop balcony was quieter than usual, softened by the amber stretch of evening light folding over the skyline. Below, the traffic hummed like static. It was constant and indifferent, reminding the team that the world moved on, even when everything inside the building felt stuck or shifting. A soft wind lifted the edge of Alex's collar, and he didn't bother to fix it.

Alex sat on the bench, a coffee cup resting between his hands, his posture loose but not relaxed. The weight of the week clung to him, not like fatigue, but like something unprocessed, something he hadn't quite found the words for. Casey sat beside him, her coffee balanced on one knee, eyes on the horizon but attention entirely on him.

He had just finished walking her through the framework: who was doing what, where the systems had bottlenecked, how Summitpoint's rigidity was slowing down collaboration. He didn't sugarcoat it. There were misalignments everywhere—tools, timelines, expectations. Still, he'd built a plan, assigned ownership, and kept things moving.

Alex glanced down at his cup, rolling it between his palms. "Thanks for the pen, by the way," he said, his voice quieter now.

Casey smiled. "Figured you needed something solid to hold onto in that office."

He chuckled, half under his breath. "It helped more than I expected."

The laughter dissolved into stillness. Casey shifted slightly to face him more directly, elbow resting on the back of the bench. "So, what's your real plan? Not the org chart version."

He took a breath and said, "Lisa's running data analysis and performance clean-up. Jordan's monitoring internal patterns—he's good at noticing where trust breaks down. Mark's keeping systems aligned and workflows mapped."

Casey nodded slowly. "Good. And what about you?"

"I'm managing the exec updates. Handling Summitpoint." He paused. "Trying to keep the pressure from spilling over."

Her eyes narrowed—not with judgment, but with curiosity. "That's delegation. But are you actually playing to their strengths—or just plugging holes?"

He blinked, then hesitated. "I mean, they're capable."

"That's not what I asked," she said gently. "You've got a team that wants to contribute. Are you putting them where there is a fire inside of them or where they won't cause fires?"

Alex sat back, thoughtful. The distinction struck him more deeply than he had expected.

"Strengths-based leadership isn't just a buzzword," Casey continued. "It's how you ignite engagement. When people work from who they are—not who they think they have to be—they stop just surviving the day. They start owning it."

He looked down again, absorbing it. "I'm trying to keep things from breaking."

"I know," she said. "But you're not here to stop failure. You're here to help them grow into what's possible."

Alex let the silence stretch. He could see Lisa's precision in analytics—Jordan's clarity under tension. Mark's quiet follow-through stabilized chaos without drawing attention. They weren't just capable. They were leaders in the making—if he made room for them to lead.

Casey tucked her hair behind one ear and leaned in slightly, her tone straightforward but sincere.

"You know, I've seen this happen on all kinds of teams—big companies, scrappy startups, it doesn't matter. The ones that really work? They stop trying to force people into roles and start letting them lean into what they're great at. It changes everything—how people show up, how they problem-solve, even how they treat each other."

She gave a small smile. "You don't need all the answers, Alex. You just need to start trusting the strengths that are already in the room."

Alex exhaled, eyes drifting to the skyline. He wasn't sure if he felt lighter, but he felt clearer. Perhaps the goal wasn't to control the entire picture, but to provide the people around him with the brushstrokes that mattered.

He looked at her and gave a quiet nod. "Alright. I'll adjust the map. Not just the tasks. The energy."

Casey smiled again, slower this time.

And for the first time in days, Alex felt like he wasn't carrying everything alone. He was building something bigger—starting with trust.

Casey tilted her head, observing him. "You know," she said, her voice softer now, "there was a time I felt like I didn't belong in rooms like this."

Alex glanced at her, curious.

She gave a small smile. "Years ago, we crossed paths in a briefing mess—you probably don't even remember. You were new to Horizon Valley. We haven't even met yet. You stood up, mid-chaos, and said, 'Leadership isn't certainty. It's courage in the middle of uncertainty.' You said it like you were trying to convince yourself. But it stuck."

She looked over at him. "Maybe you forgot. But I didn't."

He blinked, taken off guard for a beat. Then, he smiled, slow and real. "I said that?"

"You did," she said. "And I wrote it down—because it helped."

He let that settle, a flicker of humility in his expression.

Casey continued, "You're the one who made space for people to step up. Don't start shrinking now that it's your turn."

Alex looked out at the skyline again, quieter now, but more grounded. "I've been so focused on getting it right that I forgot what I already knew."

"Then remember," she said. "And lead from that place."

After a pause, Casey picked up. "Covering gaps isn't all there is to do in being a leader. It's about positioning people where they thrive. The work still needs to get done, but the difference is how—and who gets to do their best while doing it."

Alex stayed quiet, processing. She didn't rush the moment. "You don't build strong teams by plugging holes," she added.

"You build them by knowing your people well enough to put them in the right lanes—then trusting them to run."

Alex didn't respond. He didn't need to. He had stepped into the role thinking he needed to patch every crack, answer every question, and carry every piece that didn't fit cleanly. But that wasn't leadership. That was survival. And maybe it had been necessary for a time, but now the work had to change.

He looked out at the skyline. The city below kept moving—so would they. If the ground was still shifting, then the best thing he could do wasn't to stand alone but to build something steady.

Edge of the Old Pattern

The hallway outside the executive wing was quiet—too quiet. The usual churn of voices and clatter of keys had faded behind closed doors and scheduled syncs. Alex stood by the water cooler, his fingers tapping absently against a paper cup as an unread email remained open on his screen.

He should've gone straight back to the team after talking with Casey. That was the plan—head down, then return to work. But something about her words had lingered.

"You build them by knowing your people well enough to put them in the right lanes—then trusting them to run."

She wasn't wrong. But hearing it had scraped something raw. Something Alex wasn't quite ready to admit was that part of him missed the simplicity of survival mode.

Now, every decision carried more weight. Each handoff felt like a test of Alex's judgment, his authority, and his sense of self as a leader.

He stared at the flickering cursor in his inbox and almost drafted an "all-team" update himself—a script, a plan, something neat and polished to deliver before tomorrow's Summitpoint sync.

But then, he remembered what it had felt like to sit across from Howard, parsing the subtext of every word, wondering if the silence meant approval or the beginning of a takedown.

And he thought of Jordan, calm and direct on the last client call. He thought of Lisa catching a gap in the data before anyone else saw it, of Mark's careful follow-through that no one needed to double-check. They didn't need a script. They needed clarity.

He folded the paper cup quietly and dropped it in the trash. No. He wouldn't go back. Not to over-function or lead from fear. They didn't need a savior. They needed someone who could trust them.

He turned back toward the bullpen and began walking, slow but steady. Still full of doubt, but moving anyway.

DISRUPTION AND DIRECTION

The conference room still carried the residue of someone else's meeting. Half-erased bullet points curled in the margins of the whiteboard, their phrasing pure Summitpoint jargon.

- OPERATIONAL HARMONY
- COMPLIANCE CADENCE
- ZERO-DRIFT ACCOUNTABILITY

It was the kind of language that sounded strategic but landed hollow when things were breaking down.

Alex stood at the head of the table, marker in one hand, his phone face down beside him. Just before the meeting started, an email had landed—short, sharp, and tone-deaf.

ALIGN TO SUMMITPOINT STANDARDS - NO EXCEPTIONS

Trent Mallory | Director of Integration Strategy
to Alex

Horizon Valley teams are expected to adhere to standard workflows. Local preferences are noted but not prioritized. Integration requires discipline, not comfort.

Alex didn't react outwardly, but his fingers tightened slightly around the marker. He glanced at Lisa and Mark—both had seen it, too. Lisa's jaw tightened, Mark's arms crossed, eyes fixed just left of center on the whiteboard. Jordan, ever the temperature-checker, watched Alex more than anything else.

Alex broke the silence. "Let's set this up right. We can't control the org chart. But we can control how we operate and behave inside it."

Jordan raised an eyebrow. "Even if this Trent guy keeps rerouting the process through his people?"

Alex capped the marker with a quiet click. "Then we stop waiting for permission. We build a system that works—and document everything so we're ready to defend it."

He erased the remnants of buzzwords from the board with a deliberate swipe and started drawing a new workflow. "Lisa," he said, writing her name at the top of a swim lane, "you're our signal checker. Numbers, error-checking, pattern disruption. You see what others don't."

She gave a quiet nod. "That's where I'm sharpest."

"Jordan—you're our interface. Anything public-facing, executive updates, tough conversations. You don't flinch when it gets loud."

He hesitated just a beat before continuing. "Mark, you're operations. Flow, handoffs, trust leaks. Fix what breaks, and reinforce what works."

Mark looked up and said plainly, "You got it."

Lisa's lips twitched at that—small but real.

The tension didn't vanish, but it shifted. Focus replaced frustration. Postures straightened. Laptops opened. The team got to work.

Alex's phone buzzed again. A new calendar invite. Trent Mallory had scheduled a cross-functional alignment session at the same time as Alex's subsequent internal rollout. No coordination. No heads-up. No surprise.

Lisa saw it, too. She turned her laptop slightly toward him and then met his eyes. "He's trying to absorb your timeline."

Alex didn't look at the phone again. He looked at the whiteboard. At the sharp, clean lanes now labeled with actual strengths, not titles.

"If Trent wants control," Alex said quietly, "he can have the calendar. We're keeping the momentum."

The marker clicked again. Work resumed.

THE FIRST SIGNS OF CHANGE

The glass conference room carried a weight that wasn't on the agenda. Jordan sat across from Alex, both positioned with quiet purpose. Lisa and Mark flanked them, and to their left sat Alicia and Brent—operations analysts from Summitpoint Solutions. While technically assigned to support integration, they had been slow to engage and quicker to critique. Still, their presence in the room meant some kind of progress.

The organizers framed the sync with Summitpoint's leadership team as a routine check-in, but no one believed them. Now, Trent Mallory and Howard are both copied on the prep thread, but not with the phrasing in the invite: "Accountability on Integration Clarity." That wasn't a sync. It was a test.

Alex had chosen not to lead the update himself. He'd already briefed the team, mapped the key talking points, and asked Jordan to take the lead. Alex trusted him to be perfect for the task.

The speaker crackled to life as the call began. The Summitpoint director's voice came through flat and cold. "We've seen a lot of churn from your side. What exactly have you stabilized?"

Jordan didn't flinch. "We've isolated the core breakdowns—primarily in service handoffs and redundancies created by unaligned systems. We've already streamlined workflows and reassigned owners based on strengths." He nodded toward Lisa without pausing. "Lisa, you've got the numbers."

Lisa jumped in, tone crisp. "Double entry was the main time loss. We've restructured task flow and dropped reporting latency by 38% in the last 10 days. The handoffs are now tracked through shared dashboards—Horizon Valley and Summitpoint teams both have access."

There was a beat of silence. Then, the Summitpoint director responded—still measured, but something had shifted. "That's more clarity than we've gotten in any of the previous updates. Interesting."

Alex clocked the word "previous." Trent and Howard had been briefing Summitpoint separately. He'd suspected it. Now, he was hearing it.

From across the table, Alicia shifted slightly in her chair. Her eyes flicked to Brent, who gave the barest nod—skeptical, but maybe impressed. Neither said anything, and neither looked away.

The call ended without pleasantries. Summitpoint's side signed off quickly, maintaining their clipped tone, but the absence of pushback said more than any compliment would have.

Inside the room, the energy stilled, then recalibrated. Lisa exhaled slowly, and Jordan leaned back in his chair, not triumphant, but grounded. Between them passed a look of quiet acknowledgment. Mark gave a slight nod. Even Brent muttered under his breath, "Not bad," though whether it was for the numbers or the delivery was anyone's guess.

Alex stayed back, letting the team feel what they'd just done. They hadn't just updated—they had held their ground in a conversation designed to destabilize them. And they had done it without needing him to step in.

Through the glass, a shadow passed in the hallway—Howard. He didn't stop. The glance was enough to confirm what Alex already knew.

Howard had handed Trent the narrative. Alex wasn't supposed to win this moment. But he had. And now, the team knew it, too.

Alex didn't look up right away. His focus stayed on the team. They didn't flinch. *They didn't defer. And they didn't need me to step in. That's the team I've been trying to build.*

MOMENTUM BUILDS DESPITE RESISTANCE

The main office floor had changed just enough to notice at first glance. Conversations ran smoothly, updates flowed with fewer stops, and the team moved with a pace that suggested purpose.

There was still tension—mergers didn't dissolve conflict overnight—but something had begun to click. Lisa, Jordan, and Mark worked with quiet coordination, which didn't need announcements or constant course correction. There were no pep talks, no back-patting—just the shared recognition that things were beginning to work.

Across the aisle, however, the rhythm fractured. Alicia and Brent sat side by side but apart from everything else. Their presence wasn't disruptive, exactly, but it was resistant.

Alicia continued to operate in a parallel workflow and was committed to Summitpoint Solutions' reporting structures regardless of how poorly they aligned with Horizon Valley's systems. Brent rarely engaged unless someone copied Howard on the calendar invite or brought him into the room.

Earlier that morning, Brent rerouted tasks without coordinating with Lisa, following Summitpoint Solutions' legacy process instead of the one Alex's team had agreed on. The misalignment triggered a domino delay that Lisa had to fix manually—one more reminder that integration wasn't the same as cooperation.

Lisa's screen glowed with half-resolved fields and misaligned time stamps. She toggled tabs with sharp precision, tracking the issue back to its origin—Alicia had rerouted the form approval process again, bypassing the unified system they'd agreed on last week.

Lisa exhaled through her nose, not loudly, but with weight. Her fingers paused above the keyboard, then resumed typing, more deliberate now. She didn't call it out in the thread. She walked over.

Alicia sat stiffly at her desk, pulling open a Summitpoint Solutions dashboard—one that no longer synced with Horizon's workflow. Her tone of voice sharpened as she muttered something under her breath about "efficiency." Lisa didn't flinch.

She stopped just beside Alicia's chair, calm but unmoving. "You just kicked the project into a dead loop," she said, holding a printed flowchart in her hand. "We've already streamlined this twice. The third version's live—and it's the only one the client sees now."

Alicia didn't look up. "We've always handled approvals this way. It saves time."

Lisa folded the paper once and laid it on the desk between them. "Not when it breaks the handoff chain. Not when three people have to redo it after you click submit."

Alicia glanced at her. "I didn't see a thread update."

Lisa didn't miss a beat. "That's because it wasn't in the Summitpoint thread. It was in the one we all agreed on—in the channel marked 'Integration: Shared Ops.' You've been replying to the wrong one all week."

Alicia frowned, but Lisa was confident, her voice even. "We don't need another chain of command. We need accountability—and you're in the wrong thread. It's okay, we just need to own the mistake and move forward."

The room around them had quieted. Not fully, but just enough for nearby desks to catch the weight of the moment. Alicia looked away. Lisa turned back to her desk without waiting for acknowledgement.

Alicia crossed her arms, frowning at the rollout sketch.

"Your team moves fast, but the Summitpoint side hasn't signed off on this flow," she said. "We don't just go along with Horizon's systems because they're convenient."

The room quieted—tense, uncertain. Lisa glanced over but didn't step in. Jordan straightened in his chair, ready to interject.

Mark capped the marker and turned slowly toward Alicia, his expression neutral.

"We're not asking you to go along," he said, voice quiet but steady. "We're asking you to collaborate."

Alicia blinked.

Mark continued, eyes still on the diagram. "We don't need everyone to like each other yet," he added. "We just need to work together."

The words settled like a truth too grounded to argue. The room eased slightly. Lisa gave a slight, approving nod. Jordan exhaled through his nose—part relief, part respect.

Lisa sat down, refocused, and picked up where she left off—cleaning the data Alicia had just broken. But something had shifted. The next time Alicia typed, it was in the shared channel.

Alex stood back, watching. The team wasn't perfect, but it was starting to come together—focused, capable, and collaborative. Every time Summitpoint clung to old habits, the contrast sharpened. He said nothing, just let the rhythm continue. The merger was messy, but the team was starting to make sense.

JORDAN'S QUIET REVERIE

The report on Jordan's screen hadn't moved in 10 minutes. Around him, keyboards clicked, and printers hummed. The usual buzz was back—but his focus wasn't.

At Lisa's desk, she and Mark leaned over a shared spreadsheet, quietly laughing about an outdated template. Across the floor, Alicia corrected a coordinator mid-sentence. Brent muttered something dismissive, then disappeared behind his headphones.

Jordan used to admire that—certainty, control, clean lines. He'd built his reputation by staying sharp, staying silent. But something was shifting.

His gaze drifted to Alex's office. Same walls. Same bookshelves. But now, the blinds were open. A coffee mug and a whiteboard full of half-finished ideas replaced Howard's sterile order. The door hadn't closed all day.

Howard's office made you feel like you didn't belong, Jordan thought. Alex's makes you want to contribute.

His phone buzzed.

Jordan hesitated, then picked up.

"Hey Jordan," Trent said, voice smooth. "Trent Mallory, here. I just wanted to check in. If things ever start feeling murky over there, let's talk. I could use someone with your steadiness."

Jordan leaned back in his chair, eyes tracking Lisa and Mark as they worked seamlessly beside each other.

"Thanks, Trent," he said. "Appreciate the call." He didn't commit or deflect. Just left it there.

When the call ended, he stayed still for a moment, watching the floor move around him. His team—imperfect, gritty, real—was finding rhythm. He didn't know what came next. But for the first time, the idea of staying felt less like a compromise and more like a conviction.

ALEX PUSHES BACK

Howard's new office was 10 floors directly above Alex's—far enough to feel removed, close enough to loom. It was polished, minimalist, and perfectly engineered for control: glass desk, city views, not a single paper out of place. Every decision echoed power. Every silence carried a strategy.

Alex sat across from the desk, his posture steady, controlled. He had once tried to predict Howard's rhythms. Now, he studied them less as a threat and more as a map of what not to emulate.

Howard flipped a page, eyes still down. "I've reviewed the integration update. The Summitpoint analysts say your team's underdelivering. There's concern around ownership gaps."

Alex didn't blink. "We've completed two full system cycles ahead of schedule. The only inconsistency is coming from the Summitpoint side."

Howard set the page down. "Then it's a leadership issue."

A soft knock at the door interrupted them. It opened without invitation.

Trent Mallory stepped in, Summitpoint badge clipped at a perfect angle. He smiled like he'd walked into a press conference, not a private sync.

"Hope I'm not interrupting," he said.

Howard gestured slightly. Permission granted.

Alex's pulse slowed. He knew the playbook: triangulate, isolate, control the room. Trent walked a slow arc around the glass table and settled into the empty seat next to Howard.

Trent smiled like he was in on a joke. "Hey Tiger, thought I'd drop in. Figured we should align in real-time. Your team's shift away from Summitpoint protocols is raising eyebrows."

Alex folded his hands. "We adjusted process flows based on what actually works. We were spending more time translating systems than serving clients."

Trent tilted his head. "Still. It's easier to scale when everyone follows the same framework."

Alex held his ground. "Temporarily easier. Not better now or long term. We need to remember that our clients are important to us. Honestly, this seems like busy work."

Howard said nothing, but his fingers tapped lightly against his chair's armrest—barely audible, entirely intentional.

Trent leaned back. "We'll need your alignment before next week's executive sync. No solo calls. No unilateral decisions."

"I'll bring it to my team," Alex said.

"Bring it?" Trent echoed, one eyebrow raised. "Or enforce it?"

Alex stood slowly, gaze steady. "That depends on whether it helps us do better work—or just look more compliant."

The silence was razor-thin. Howard didn't move. Trent gave a smile and a faint nod, the kind that didn't signal agreement—just acknowledged that someone had drawn the lines.

As Alex left, he didn't look back.

In the hallway, He stood, calm and deliberate, and turned toward the elevator without waiting for a closing word. The door closed behind him with a soft hiss of compressed air, leaving the pristine silence behind.

Back with the team, the energy felt different. The constant movement of people kept the floor from staying polished to a shine. Lisa stood at Mark's desk, walking through a process fix. Jordan coordinated with two other departments on a shared call schedule. Alicia sat upright, eyes fixed on her screen, typing without engaging. Brent scrolled through a spreadsheet, headphones in, disconnected from the quiet motion around him.

Alex strolled through the space. The rhythm wasn't perfect yet, but it was real. There was friction and movement, questions, and follow-through. His office door remained open—it had been all day.

His office is higher and dead silent, he thought. *But down here, we're building something real. Something that listens, flexes, and grows.*

Chapter 8

Crossfire

It was now time for the Summitpoint Solutions and Horizon Valley Leadership sync meeting. The previous day's interactions with Howard and Trent had exhausted Alex, but he focused on creating an environment where his team could thrive and collaborate. He made his way up to the executive conference room.

Designers built the executive conference room on the 12th floor to impress with floor-to-ceiling windows, a smoked glass table, and a lighting system that adjusted every 15 minutes to reduce "decision fatigue." Today, it felt like a trap.

Alex arrived 10 minutes early. At the far end of the room sat Trent Mallory, immaculately put together, thumbs scrolling through a report he didn't need to read. Across from him, Howard stood near the whiteboard, marker in hand but unmoving. Alex could feel his heart drop. He took a breath.

"Alex," Howard said, with a tone that was technically a greeting. "Have a seat."

He did. The chair felt colder than the room.

Trent didn't look up. "Hey, Tiger. I did some checking around after our chat yesterday. We've had conflicting reports about the rollout timeline," he said. "Your internal team claimed the integration milestone had been cleared. But my operations lead says the client-facing dashboards are still using the Horizon format."

"They are," Alex replied evenly. "Because we haven't resolved the field compatibility in the Summitpoint template yet. Switching early would've created more errors."

Trent finally met his eyes. "Then why was it marked complete in the last update?"

Alex turned to Howard. "That came from your office. The draft summary was approved before we'd finalized the audit."

Howard didn't flinch. "I assumed your team would clean up the remaining pieces after submission. We needed to show momentum."

There it was—deflection by delegation.

Trent folded his hands. "So, let me get this straight. Your team submitted incomplete data, and no one corrected it?"

Alex's jaw tightened, but his voice stayed calm. "My team flagged the risk. Someone else pushed it, though."

Howard cut in, tone diplomatic but sharp-edged. "What you were told was to keep pace with the integration benchmarks. We can't afford delays that make us look divided."

Alex let the silence stretch. "We're already divided, Trent. That's the problem. You're trying to enforce top-down systems without understanding the existing structure. Whenever your team ignores the workflows we're building, we lose ground."

Trent's expression didn't shift, but his tone cooled. "What you call friction, I call correction. You're leading from sentiment, not scale."

"I'm leading from what works," Alex said. "And what works is building trust before you expect compliance."

Howard stepped in, casual but performative. "We're not here to debate philosophy. We need clarity on who owns the next milestone."

There it was—the throw under the bus, neatly folded in executive lingo.

Trent leaned forward. "If your team can't meet alignment standards in the next cycle, we'll reassign system leadership to Summitpoint ops. Agreed?"

Howard said nothing. He didn't need to. The silence was consent.

Alex nodded once, slowly. "Understood."

He didn't argue. Not here. But he made a silent note: *This wasn't about control but character, and today revealed both.*

As the meeting wrapped, Trent gathered his notes, already texting on his way out. Howard didn't offer a nod or closing remark—just walked out like it had been another item checked off.

Alex sat a beat longer. The windows stretched the skyline across the glass table like a mirror, but all he saw was the reflection of two leaders more concerned with optics than people.

He stood, spine straight, and walked out.

QUIET VICTORIES

Evening settled across the Horizon Valley floor, softening the hum of screens and fluorescent lights. People had cleared most desks, let monitors fall asleep, and rinsed and turned mugs upside down. But Alex's team remained in motion—not in a rush, not out of obligation—but because they wanted to finish what they'd started.

Music drifted from someone's phone—soft indie beats, barely above a whisper. The playlist had already rotated through three different genres, but no one had turned it off. The whiteboard near the breakroom was no longer a mess of scribbles—it had become a patchwork of hand-drawn emojis, "Ask Mark About the Printer" jokes, and Lisa's running list of "Small Wins," updated with a new sticky note labeled: "Summitpoint call = done with a smiley face."

Lisa sat cross-legged on a spare chair, a cookie in one hand, her laptop perched on her knees. Jordan reclined nearby, texting while he balanced a cold can of soda on the armrest. Mark stood with two ops leads at the whiteboard, rewriting a workflow loop without being asked. A half-empty container of chocolate-covered almonds passed between them.

Alex leaned on the edge of his desk, quietly scanning Jordan's latest status update, not because he needed to micromanage it, but because he liked seeing the tone—confident, sharp, owned.

What made this different wasn't productivity but presence. That's when Alicia appeared. She hovered by the breakroom doorway, coffee in hand, eyes drifting across the floor. Brent followed a few paces behind, moving slower and more guardedly. Neither said anything. Not yet.

Mark noticed first. "We're still testing version three of the integrated workflow," he said, addressing Lisa but loud enough for others to hear. "Less redundancy. More logic."

Lisa gestured toward her screen. "You want to jump in?" Her question was casual, directed toward no one in particular.

Alicia stepped closer. She didn't sit, but her eyes narrowed as she scanned the visuals. "You layered Summitpoint's milestone framework into Horizon's system timeline?"

Lisa nodded, casually popping the last bite of her cookie. "Yep. Took two extra hours, but it holds."

Alicia said nothing for a beat. "That's not what the rollout plan asked for."

"Nope," Jordan said, lifting his can. "But it's the only thing that worked."

Brent gave a slow exhale. "It's cleaner than what we've been running."

Alex didn't interrupt. He let the moment play.

Without glancing up, Lisa added, "We're not trying to replace everything. Just make the new thing work."

Alicia stepped a little closer. "Have you logged the framework yet?"

Mark turned from the board. "We just started mapping it into the shared documentation. Want to see it?"

She hesitated. "Send it to me. I'll take it into tomorrow's sync."

Brent gave a quiet nod. "Loop me in, too. I'll make sure it doesn't get buried."

Alex finally spoke. "Appreciate that. This doesn't work if it only lives in our corner."

Alicia's brow twitched slightly, almost a smile. "We're not in opposite corners anymore."

She didn't linger. She and Brent moved on, but they hadn't dismissed it—not this time. They left behind two half-empty mugs on the side table—one of them beside the cookie plate.

Lisa raised her eyebrows as the door swung shut behind them. "Did they just... fold in?"

Mark cracked a rare smile. "Skeptical. But engaged."

Jordan looked at Alex. "Progress."

Alex didn't say anything, but he felt it. The team hadn't set or finalized the culture yet. But something had shifted—from survival to ownership, from silos to slow trust. Not loud. Not dramatic.

From the hallway, Casey paused just outside the glass wall of the bullpen. She didn't step in, didn't interrupt—just stood for a moment, watching through the frame. Alex was leaning casually against a desk, Mark sketching on the whiteboard, while Lisa and Jordan were mid-discussion, their sleeves rolled up and postures relaxed.

Even Alicia and Brent hovered nearby, neither team nor outsiders. The whole floor hummed—not with urgency, but with rhythm.

Casey smiled to herself, small and genuine. *He's not just leading, she thought. He's building something real.*

REFLECT

1. What's the difference between surviving leadership and practicing it? How do you know when you're reacting versus truly leading?
2. Have you ever stepped into a leadership role with inherited dynamics you didn't choose? How did you manage the challenges that came with the space?
3. Who on your team shows quiet strengths that might not align with titles or org charts? Are you creating room for them to lead in their own way?
4. When do you feel most like a contributor, and when do you feel most like a placeholder? What changes those dynamics?

5. Do you recognize small moments of culture-building, or do you only look for big wins? What signals do you pay attention to in team cohesion?

6. What does it mean to create a culture where people can exhale? How do you help foster that feeling of safety and shared ownership?

ACTION

1. How can you map your team's current responsibilities to their actual strengths this week? Who might be underused—or misused?

2. What one process or habit can you change that better aligns with a strengths-based approach? Who can help me lead that change?

3. Leave your door open—literally or metaphorically—for the next week. Notice how that one small change impacts the way people approach you.

4. Delegate one responsibility you've been holding onto—not because others can't handle it, but because you haven't let go yet.

5. Invite your team to co-write part of your next meeting agenda. Include space for the members' insights, not just your updates.

6. Choose one legacy process you've kept because "that's how it's always been." Challenge yourself to ask, "Is this still serving the team?"

Alex,

For someone who finally stopped asking for permission. Never let anyone dismiss your strengths.

-Casey

CHAPTER 9

Empowering Others

The Ripple Effect

Great things are not done by impulse, but by a series of small things brought together."

-Vincent van Gogh

The hum of Horizon Valley on Monday morning no longer sounded like chaos. Sunlight stretched across the open floor, softening the buzz of conversation. The team had stabilized the client project, and the reports were clean and accurate. Upper management seemed satisfied—for now. It should've felt like a win. But something in the air said otherwise.

Voices stayed low, and movement was cautious. Alicia and Brent lingered on the periphery, watching others enter meetings that excluded them. And Howard, once distant, had started showing up in huddles, reviewing timelines, and asking “curious” questions that made people second-guess themselves. It was not overt interference—just enough to pull focus.

Near the break room, Lisa leaned against the counter, arms crossed, coffee untouched. Jordan stood beside her, scanning the room. They knew the difference between momentum and manipulation. They could feel things shifting.

Alex stepped off the elevator, already running through his day: project checkpoints, syncs, and an intern handoff from HR.

But when he saw Lisa and Jordan approaching with quiet urgency, he stopped mid-step. He didn't have to ask. Their expressions said everything. What mattered now wasn't schedules or task lists—it was the team.

A UNITED FRONT

Lisa and Jordan closed in on Alex in the hallway near the break room. The air was tight—stiff postures, sharp eyes, no trace of humor left. Alex had just grabbed his coffee when Lisa stepped directly into his path, not with her usual teasing grin but with a quiet force, saying this wasn't just about frustration—it was about strategy now.

"We need to talk," Lisa said, low but firm. Her glance toward Alex's office was enough. Not here. Eyes lingered in the hallway, and Alicia had just stepped out of a meeting with Brent, both now within earshot. Whatever this was, it wasn't for the open floor.

Alex nodded and turned without a word. The three of them walked briskly toward his office. Brent looked up just as they passed, watching them go without comment.

Once inside, Alex closed the door, but neither Lisa nor Jordan took a seat. They stood flanking the desk like sentinels.

He broke the silence first. "What's going on?"

Lisa didn't waste time. "Howard asked Brent for a version of our last report," she said. "Privately. He called it a 'secondary validation,' but he left your name off the request."

Alex stiffened, the coffee forgotten in his hand.

Jordan picked it up from there, his tone low but edged. "And Alicia said he's been forwarding notes from our stand-ups to Trent. So, he can make his annotations." He met Alex's eyes. "He's not just watching anymore. He's waiting for a crack."

Lisa stepped closer, voice sharper now. "He's undermining from above without leaving fingerprints. And the worst part? Brent didn't think to question it. He just handed it over."

Alex exhaled slowly, jaw tight. "Did you confront him?"

Lisa shook her head. "Not yet. We brought it to you first."

Jordan nodded. "Because if this keeps up, it doesn't matter what kind of culture we're building. One whisper from ten floors up, and it all starts to unravel."

Alex ran a hand across the edge of his desk, grounding himself. He'd known Howard was circling—had felt it in the syncs, the call reassignments, the sudden visibility. But this? Howard's moves were more deliberate than Alex had realized.

Jordan added, calmer now, but with a resolve that filled the room: "Whatever's coming next, we're with you. But we have to do it our way. Not his."

Lisa's tone softened, but not her certainty. "We've been more engaged in the last two months than in the last two years. This works, Alex. But we can't defend it alone."

Alex looked at both of them, the weight of their words settling into his spine, not like a burden, but like armor. He'd been leading, yes. But this was different.

What they offered wasn't just support—this was allegiance. Together, they were drawing the line.

MEETING THE INTERN

The HR conference room was still and impersonal—a polished table, clean carpet, and a tray of untouched pastries more for show than use. Alex had just stepped out of a team huddle when the message came.

Inside, the HR manager stood beside a sharp-eyed young woman in her early 20s, shoulders squared, posture practiced. Her name was Rylie, and she was a student rotating through various departments before deciding where to settle. For the next few weeks, she'd be with his team.

"This is Alex," the HR manager said warmly, gesturing toward him. "You will be with his team the next couple of weeks."

Rylie's head lifted quickly. "Oh, hey—nice to meet you," she said, her voice clipped and polite, trying to sound confident but not say the wrong thing.

Alex gave her a relaxed, easy, and unforced smile. "Nice to meet you, too. First, I will connect you with Lisa and Mark. They will help you get going in the department."

She gave a slight nod, something between acknowledgment and relief. "Okay. Thanks."

As HR wrapped up, Alex felt the shift was more than another intern rotation. He wasn't the new one anymore. He was now a mentor, shaping the space instead of trying to fit into it.

He thought of Casey—how she had led with curiosity, not control. She'd given him space to grow without rushing him. Now, it was his turn to do the same.

Rylie gathered her materials, quiet but composed, her eyes flicking around the room as if she were still unsure if she belonged. Alex noticed. She had come to learn, but he'd make sure she felt seen. More than a seat at the table, she needed to know her voice mattered.

LEADERSHIP THAT BUILDS BELONGING

The conference room carried the usual buzz of setup—laptops opening, chairs scooting into place, low chatter as the team settled in. Lisa flipped through the shared agenda while Jordan adjusted the monitor cable for the screen projection. Mark sat with his usual quiet focus, already a few lines into the notes.

At the far edge of the table, Rylie hovered just outside the rhythm of it all. She had sat near the corner, notebook open and pen in hand, but she hadn't written anything yet. Her shoulders were still stiff, eyes darting between faces, unsure whether she was here to observe or contribute, or whether speaking at all would mark her overstepping.

The room was friendly, but Rylie hadn't found her place. She listened as Lisa walked the group through the workflow overview, occasionally nodding but never speaking a word. Her notebook remained mostly blank.

Alex caught it out of the corner of his eye. She leaned in, fully engaged. She was studying the team's cadence, trying to map out where she fit, as if there might be some unspoken rule about when an intern was allowed to speak. He paused mid-sentence, barely noticeable to the rest of the group, and shifted his attention toward her.

"Alright, Rylie," he said casually, folding his hands on the table. "What do you think?"

Her head jerked up slightly. "Me?"

Jordan grinned across the table. "Yeah, new kid. Sink or swim."

Lisa nudged him with an elbow, her voice sharp enough to sting. "Ignore him. You're part of this team now."

Alex didn't push. He kept his tone warm but steady, giving Rylie space. "Seriously, fresh perspective is valuable. What stands out to you?"

Rylie hesitated, then glanced down at her notes. Her pen hovered briefly over the page before circling something near the bottom. She didn't look up immediately, but her voice came clearer than expected.

"The reporting dashboard delay," she began. "It's not a system error. I think the category tags aren't matching—the naming's inconsistent between datasets."

For a beat, the room froze. Then, Lisa blinked, eyebrows lifting. "That would explain the data drift."

Jordan leaned forward, impressed. "You just solved something we've been chasing for days."

Mark gave a low whistle, already pulling up his laptop. "Let me check that now."

A hum of energy sparked around the table—heads nodding, notes scribbling, the momentum that only comes from a shared breakthrough.

Except for Alicia. She crossed one leg over the other and spoke without turning her head. "If that's the case, it should've been flagged by operations, not the intern."

The air tightened. Rylie's shoulders dipped slightly, her pen lowering to the table. The ripple of encouragement paused.

Jordan's grin faded. Lisa glanced at Alex, her expression unreadable but alert.

Alex didn't wait. "Intern or not," he said, his tone calm but direct, "she's part of the team. And she spotted something we missed."

Alicia shrugged, eyes still on her screen. "Just saying—there's a process. Howard wouldn't want people jumping the line."

Alex leaned in just slightly. "And I want people to be empowered and encouraged to speak up when they see something valuable. That's our process."

Alicia didn't argue. She sat back, arms crossed, the edge still in her posture, but the sharpness in her tone had dulled. She gave a single, slow nod, more measured than defiant.

Alex turned back to the table as Lisa leaned toward Rylie. "Nice work," she said simply. "Let's build that into the next update."

Jordan nodded in agreement. "Seriously, solid catch."

Mark added without looking up, "This'll clean up half the reporting lag."

Rylie didn't say much. But her nod back was firmer. She stayed quiet for the rest of the meeting but was different now—more anchored, more engaged. Her notebook filled steadily, her pen moving with purpose.

Alex saw the shift. It wasn't loud. No applause, no fanfare. Just a change in posture. A sharper presence. The ripple had begun and already reached the table's edge.

TESTING LOYALTIES

The afternoon at Horizon Valley moved with quiet purpose. Lisa and Mark stood at the whiteboard, trading edits mid-sentence. Across the aisle, Jordan coached a teammate through a calendar fix. It wasn't flashy—just steady, collaborative work. The team moved like they trusted each other.

Alicia stood nearby, arms crossed, watching. Brent flipped through a printout, but his eyes were on the room. "It's weird," he murmured. "No one's angling for credit."

Alicia didn't answer right away. Her gaze stayed on Lisa and Mark. "It won't last," she said. "Too many moving parts."

"Or maybe," Brent said, folding the paper, "they've figured something out."

They both glanced at Rylie, focused on her desk. Brent approached. "Rylie, right? That dashboard catch—nice work."

Rylie looked up, calm. "Thanks. Just a mismatch. Lisa already had most of it."

Alicia offered a small smile. "Still. Most interns don't jump in like that."

"I didn't think about it," Rylie said. "Alex said everyone has a voice. So, I used mine."

Brent nodded, surprised by her clarity. Lisa passed by, tapping Rylie's desk with a quick "good job" as she moved on.

"They make it easy," Rylie added. "No competition. Just teamwork."

Brent chuckled. "Very not-Summitpoint."

Alicia was quiet. Then, softly: "Howard ran it the same way. Direct. No need for debate."

Brent glanced over, surprised at her honesty. Alicia just watched the whiteboard, where Lisa and Mark worked like a team, fluid and balanced, with no one posturing.

As Rylie returned to her notes, Alicia and Brent returned to their desks—quiet, thoughtful. Their skepticism hadn't vanished, but something had shifted. They weren't dismissing it anymore. They were considering it.

MARK AND RYLIE WORK TOGETHER

The team worked with quiet intention, wrapping up before the last stretch of the afternoon. Lisa and Jordan met with a client at the far end of the floor while Alex continued his leadership check-in in the executive suite.

Rylie stood at the whiteboard near her desk, puzzling over a small process flow. She had drafted two versions—both logical and clean—but couldn't decide which would integrate better into the shared workflow. Her eyes flicked between the diagrams, uncertainty pulling at her brow.

Mark walked past with a handful of printed reports, paused, and tilted his head toward the board. "Trying to reinvent the wheel?" he asked, quiet but kind.

"Trying not to break it," Rylie replied with a slight grin. "I can't tell if the simpler option misses something."

Mark set his papers down and looked at both diagrams, nodding slowly. "This one," he said, pointing to her second option. "It leaves more room for conversation. Fewer assumptions baked in."

Rylie blinked. "You got that from two arrows and a label?"

Mark shrugged lightly and said, "Insights come from experience. Also, it's okay to break the wheel. It's just a wheel."

She smiled, and something in her shoulders relaxed slightly more than before. Mark picked up his reports again, offered a brief nod, and walked off—nothing too dramatic, but a simple connection.

Strength in Support

Casey's office didn't look like an executive suite. No oversized desk. No sleek nameplate. A round table surrounded by mismatched chairs and a wall of color-coded Post-its—names, roles, strengths, projects—arranged more by momentum than hierarchy. Framed personal and company photos lined the back wall.

A junior staffer stepped in briefly with an update, then left without pause or pretense, just ease. Alex watched it happen and felt a quiet shift in his chest. It wasn't envy but admiration.

"You've built something here," he said.

Casey leaned back in her chair, relaxed. "Took long enough. But yeah—it's sticking."

He nodded, fingertips brushing the edge of the table. "Lisa and Jordan came to me this morning. Said they're in—as long as I don't start leading like Howard."

Casey's smile turned knowing. "That's the thing about trust. Once people experience it, they'll do everything they can to protect it."

Alex exhaled, then added, "Howard's still finding workarounds—Alicia, Brent. Quiet nudges. Subtle redirects."

Casey's expression didn't change. "And yet, Alicia didn't escalate the last meeting. Brent's asking more questions than giving orders."

Alex hesitated. "The intern, Rylie, said something to them, actually. First hour with the team. Caught a data issue we all missed."

Casey's brows lifted. "Did she?"

"Yeah. Small fix. But it landed. Brent even thanked her," he answered.

Casey leaned forward slightly. "That's what empowerment looks like. Leadership isn't just about making room for the ones who agree with you. It's about inviting every voice to the table—especially the ones still finding theirs."

Alex glanced toward her whiteboard, taking in the scribbled strengths and color-coded names. "Feels familiar," he said. "I was Rylie once. Nervous. Trying not to get in the way."

Casey gave him a teasing glance. "Please. You were never not in the way."

He laughed. "I don't know; I felt like it at first. But you encouraged me and didn't rush me. I'm trying to do the same for her."

Casey nodded, more serious now. "That's how culture sticks. Not through command. Through consistency. People first, always."

Alex leaned back, arms folding loosely. "Whatever Howard's playing at, I think I'm past caring. We've got something real now."

Casey's voice softened. "Look at you. Leading people who lead others."

They sat for a beat in quiet understanding. What once was mentor and mentee had shifted. Now, it was a shared knowing between two leaders shaping from the inside, not controlling from above.

As Alex stood to leave, his phone buzzed—a message from Howard's office

There was no context, no warning.

He glanced at the screen, then back at Casey, brcathcd, and pocketed the phone. This time, he wasn't walking in alone.

Chapter 9

The Culture Speaks

The conference room felt more like a stage. A polished table ran the length of it, flanked by high-backed chairs and tense silence. Papers rustled, a pen clicked, a chair adjusted. Sunlight sliced across the surface in narrow bands. It was mid-morning, but the weight in the air said otherwise.

Howard stood at the head of the table, arms loose, hands clasped. He didn't speak. His presence alone signaled that this wasn't just another sync but a test.

Alex sat halfway down the left side, steady and quiet. Lisa, Jordan, and Mark clustered nearby—a familiar rhythm. Across from them, Alicia and Brent sat composed and unreadable. The seating wasn't random. Howard had drawn the lines.

When Howard finally spoke, his voice was smooth and deliberate. "Let's refocus on priorities. We've spent too much time circling feedback loops and peer review rituals. It's inefficient. What we need is clear decision-making and top-down accountability."

Alex didn't blink. "We've been delivering because people feel ownership—not because someone's managing every move."

Howard's eyes narrowed just slightly. "You've created an environment where everyone feels entitled to weigh in. That's not always a strength."

Lisa leaned in, her tone even but direct. "And yet, it's working. People aren't afraid to speak—and that's by design."

Jordan said calmly, "If we need proof, the metrics speak for themselves. We can pull them up now."

Mark gave a single, quiet nod. He didn't need words—his presence carried weight.

Howard let the silence stretch a beat longer than needed, then tapped a pen lightly against the table. "You know," he said, glancing toward the others, "this culture of empowerment—that came from the top. I set the foundation. What you're seeing now is just the next phase."

Alex didn't look away. "Then I hope you see how strong it's become now that people are actually trusted to lead."

Howard's eyes drifted down the table. "Brent, your perspective?"

Brent hesitated, then met Howard's look briefly before shifting to Alex. "Honestly? Things are smoother. Collaboration's real. It's quieter—but more productive."

A tiny flicker passed over Howard's face, long enough to catch.

He turned to Alicia. "Your take?"

Alicia paused, then spoke with care. "I had my doubts. But people are talking. Solving problems together. It's not chaotic—it's starting to work."

There was a shift in the room—subtle, but undeniable. The tension didn't vanish, but it softened, like a thread had loosened just enough for people to exhale. Even Howard seemed to register it. He tapped a finger once against the table, then turned to the next slide in his deck without comment.

Alex observed him. He knew Howard had positioned Alicia and Brent here as quiet reinforcement—pressure disguised as participation. Instead of bolstering control, they validated something else entirely: the culture taking root under Alex's leadership. They hadn't defended the old way. They'd told the truth.

Alex sat back a little, his expression unreadable, but something shifted behind his eyes. Howard had set a stage meant to corner him. But the moment never came. The team hadn't fractured. They aligned.

The meeting rolled on—metrics, schedules, next steps—but it felt different. No one raised their voice. No one needed to. The power play hadn't landed. And when the session wrapped, the win was quiet, but unmistakable.

Howard still held the title, but the center of influence was shifting. Alicia and Brent—whether they realized it or not—had stepped toward that shift. They weren't challenging authority, and they weren't standing apart. They were starting to act like teammates. Not entirely inside the circle yet, but no longer on the outside. And that momentum was enough.

The Ripple Effect

Late afternoon at Horizon Valley brought a quiet rhythm back to the main floor. The earlier tension from the department sync had dissolved into something calmer and more grounded. People were back at their desks, heads down, but the silence was focused and intentional. The kind of silence that spoke more to trust than caution.

Alex stood in the open space between his office and the bullpen, sipping from a mug of coffee that had long since gone lukewarm. He didn't mind. The warmth in the room was coming from the people.

Lisa sat beside Rylie, pointing at her screen and letting her take the mouse and explore the reporting tool herself. She guided her without hovering, patient but expectant. Rylie asked questions occasionally, but her hands moved more confidently as she typed, tested, and tried again.

The team moved fluidly now, a rhythm of collaboration settling in. Rylie leaned over her keyboard as she adjusted a tagging template based on feedback from Lisa.

Brent passed behind her, a folder under one arm, and tapped her desk. "Keep up the good work."

Rylie smiled in return, just enough to acknowledge the praise without overstating it.

Across the room, Alicia looked up from her screen. The moment had been quick, almost nothing, but her eyes followed Brent. Her lips pressed into a line. Her expression was neutral, but it looked like she was quietly processing. She returned to her screen without saying a word.

Alicia crossed behind Lisa and handed her a packet of data sheets. "Cleaned the tags," she said casually. "Should match your dashboard now."

Lisa blinked, surprised, but nodded and filed the update without fuss.

Alex didn't move. He just watched—people reaching across lines, solving problems without waiting for permission. The team wasn't asking to lead. They already were.

Leadership used to feel like something he had to hold. Now, it felt like something he had to pass on.

Behind him, the light from his office cast a faint glow. The door stayed open—just as he intended. As he turned, Rylie looked up and met his eyes across the room, offering a quiet smile.

He returned it. What started as his risk had become their rhythm. It belonged to all of them now, shifting the culture, one ripple at a time.

RYLIE AND ALEX

Later that week, Rylie hovered near Alex's office door after the team meeting had cleared out. She tucked her notebook under one arm, her brows tightening in thought. Alex looked up from his screen and offered an easy nod.

"Got a question?" he asked, setting his pen down.

She stepped in, hesitant but focused. "Sort of. It's not about the dashboard or sales. Not directly, anyway."

Alex gestured to the open seat. "Shoot."

She sat, leaning forward just slightly. "I've worked in a few departments now. Seen a lot of managers—a lot of teams." She paused. "But this one's different. People actually talk. They ask for help and challenge each other, without getting weird about it. It's not competitive or fearful. Why is it so different here?"

Alex smiled faintly, leaning forward. "It's because we trust each other. Relationships are more important than problems."

Rylie's head tilted, intrigued.

"We've all worked in places where silence was the safest move," Alex continued. "Where speaking up made you a target or put you on someone's radar for the wrong reasons. This team? We work better when people bring their whole selves to the table. That only happens when they trust they won't be punished for trying."

Rylie nodded, her eyes reflective. "It's weird how new that feels."

"It shouldn't be," Alex said. "But it is. That's why we protect it."

PASS IT ON

The hallway outside Alex's office was quiet now, illuminated by the warm glow of evening lights. Most of the floor had emptied, but the energy hadn't drained—it had simply settled. The kind of quiet that follows good work, not exhaustion.

Alex stepped out, coffee in hand, just in time to see Casey rounding the corner toward the elevator, her bag over one shoulder.

"Heading out?" he asked, falling into step beside her.

"Finally," she said with a slight grin. "You?"

"Trying to," he said, then gestured over his shoulder. "But they don't really need me anymore."

Casey paused, turning to glance at the bullpen behind him. Rylie and Lisa sat side by side reviewing a dashboard update. Jordan and Mark were laughing over a whiteboard sketch that had become serious and ridiculous. Brent stood nearby, asking clarifying questions. Alicia leaned on the divider, arms crossed, but listening. No one looked at Alex. And that was the point.

Casey smiled, then looked back at him. "You didn't build a team that needs you. You built one that leads without you."

Alex gave a quiet nod. "It's strange. I used to think leadership was about being the one with the answers. Now it feels more like clearing space so others can step forward."

"Exactly," she said. "You stopped proving yourself. And started empowering others to do the same."

They reached the elevator. Casey stepped inside as the doors slid open, but turned before they closed.

"Keep doing that," she said, eyes warm. "Keep giving it away."

Alex held her gaze. "Every day."

The doors closed, and Alex stood momentarily, sipping his lukewarm coffee. The floor behind him hummed—not with tension, but with momentum. The kind that didn't start with him—and wouldn't end with him either.

He turned, not to oversee, but to walk through the space and check in—not as a supervisor, but as someone invested in how far others could go.

Leadership wasn't his to hold anymore. It was his to pass on.

Reflect

1. What does it mean to truly empower someone, especially when they're new, hesitant, or different from you?
2. Are you the kind of mentor you once needed—or are you still waiting for someone to validate your place?

3. What kind of culture have you contributed to—intentionally or unintentionally—through your actions? How do you know?

4. When was your last pause to acknowledge quiet leadership, not from titles but from contribution? Are there individuals on your team who might be waiting for permission to contribute more fully? What signs are you missing?

5. What does it look like when leadership is shared instead of centralized in your context?

6. How do you respond with curiosity or correction when someone speaks a hard truth (like Rylie or Jordan)?

ACTION

1. Who on your team has been quietly contributing—and how can you spotlight their impact this week?

2. Reflect on your current approach to decision-making. Where can you invite more shared ownership without sacrificing clarity?

3. How can you model open-door leadership—physically, emotionally, and culturally?

4. Who might be watching from the edges, like Rylie once was? What action will you take to include them?

5. Pick one behavior you've seen from a peer or team member that models the culture you want to build. Name it out loud. Practice it.
6. What's one small way you can create more psychological safety in your next team meeting?
7. In the next week, what's one thing you can do to show that trust, not fear, holds this team together?

Dear Alex,

Keep giving it away.

From, Casey

CHAPTER 10

LEADERSHIP AS A JOURNEY

Leadership begins in the quiet moments of honest reflection."

-Susan Scott

The floor was still mostly dark. Motion lights flickered on in slow, staggered intervals—first near the entrance, then over by the elevators, one after the other like the building hadn't decided to wake up yet. Outside, the city was beginning to stir—delivery vans easing into curb lanes, steam curling from vents, traffic lights blinking their steady rhythm. Inside, it was quieter and intentional.

Casey sat at her round table, not behind her desk. She never liked the way a desk felt like a barrier. She believed strategy worked best at eye level. The table held a journal, a black pen, and a mug that read “Create > Control”—a gift from an intern who’d taken three extra weeks to stay in her department.

Her posture was relaxed, but her focus wasn’t on the whiteboard. The left wall, usually loud with sticky notes, arrows, and Q2 campaign metrics, could wait. Her attention was elsewhere—on her laptop screen, an old email open and enlarged.

Alex	Thinking about walking away	2:17 am

She reread it—not for content, but for contrast. Alex didn’t walk away, she thought. He walked through. And he’s still walking. That’s what leadership looks like when you stop pretending it’s about having all the answers.

She picked up the pen and wrote a few more lines beneath the journal heading.

Lessons I Wish I’d Learned Earlier

You don’t grow out of doubt. You learn to lead beside it.
Control feels safe. But trust builds momentum.
Progress doesn’t always feel like clarity. Sometimes, it feels like humility.
Power isn’t what you hold—it’s what you’re trusted to give away.

A light knock on the glass pulled her out of the thought. Mia stepped in, portfolio binder in one hand, can of matcha in the other. She was grinning to herself. She knew her boss would be in this early.

"Didn't realize VPs had office hours that started before sunrise," she said.

Casey didn't look up. "Only when the creative brief and Q2 budget review both show up on the same day."

Mia placed the binder on the table. "Analytics reports came in early. Digital's CTRs are up, but Summitpoint's campaign spend blew through the ceiling. Signature's already on the approval."

Casey pointed to the table. "Drop it here. Flag it for the 10:00 AM check-in—I want eyes on the backend before I escalate anything."

Mia nodded. "Got it. Oh—and there's a message for you. Wants a second opinion on the internal messaging draft before pushing it live. Didn't say it, but it's a 'Casey, tell me if I'm overdoing it' kind of message."

Casey smirked. "People are learning the art of the soft ask. It's progress."

Mia tilted her head, watching her a second longer than usual. "Have you ever thought about how many people are leading because of the room you made for them?"

Casey didn't answer right away. Her voice was quieter when she did. "All the time. I am glad to be part of their stories. "

Mia lingered another second, then backed toward the door. "You need anything else?"

Casey didn't hesitate. "Just a reminder in an hour: Review the draft, and pretend I'm not five projects behind."

Mia grinned. "Copy that. VP of Strategic Delusion, at your service."

Casey looked toward the corner of her whiteboard as the door clicked shut. A single yellow sticky note, slightly faded. Bold handwriting.

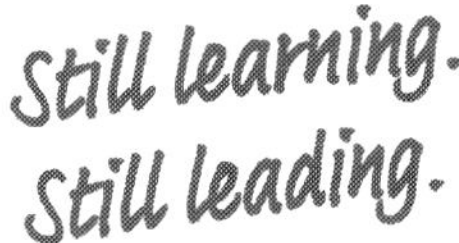

She tapped it once. It's a habit. And whenever she does it, it feels like a reset. Then, she closed her journal, picked up the binder, and got to work.

Just as Casey reached for her tablet, her phone buzzed against the table's edge—an unfamiliar number lit the screen. She hesitated. People usually ignored early calls from unknown sources. But instinct overruled routine, and she picked it up.

It was Xander Jay.

The newly elected chairman of the board. Charismatic, media-savvy, and already shaping internal conversations with his public-facing charm and behind-the-scenes curiosity. He didn't typically reach out directly, especially not to VPs.

Whatever this was, it wasn't routine.

Casey sat back, spine straightening as she listened, her coffee growing cold beside the journal she had just closed. No agenda, no pleasantries—just a request for perspective. Off the record.

She reached again for her pen. *Some conversations we should not forget.*

Chapter 10

Alex's Morning Walk and Self-Audit

The park wasn't far—just across the service lane behind Horizon Valley's main building. But it always felt like a different city—a softer one. Concrete benches ringed a clean rectangle of grass, the kind that looked more curated than used. Trees marked the corners—symmetrical, planned. Nothing wild here, nothing unexpected. But it was quiet, and that was enough.

He walked the perimeter slowly, jacket unbuttoned, a half-crumpled breakfast sandwich wrapper in his hand. He passed a pair of pigeons near a bench and didn't notice them until they fluttered away. His thoughts weren't loud, but they were persistent. They often were in places like this—neutral spaces that held no meetings, no metrics, just time.

Alex crossed to a shaded bench near the edge of a raised planter and sat down. The quiet didn't ask anything from him. It just allowed space.

He pulled the black notebook from his inner pocket. Its spine had softened. A few pages were dog-eared, most from moments like this. He flipped through past coaching notes, half-finished to-dos, and clipped insights from team check-ins. When he reached a clean page, he didn't start right away. Instead, he let his eyes linger on the blankness—the permission to ask without answering.

What am I still unlearning?

Where am I hiding instead of showing up?

How do I want people to describe my leadership when I'm not in the room?

He stopped and listened.

Behind him, a breeze moved through the hedges, carrying the scent of flatbread from the food truck. Across the path, two junior employees sat on the low ledge, voices low but clear enough to reach him between bites.

"I'd take clear expectations over 'cool boss' energy any day."

"Just tell me what success looks like."

"I've had three managers this year. None of them would manage."

"Being direct felt like a social crime."

"I don't need perfect. Just real."

The laughter that followed wasn't cruel—it was the kind that releases something. Alex didn't write any of it down. He didn't need to. Those truths had already made a place in him.

He glanced back at the notebook and added one final line.

Am I leading with intention, or just avoiding imperfection?

He tapped the pen once, a quiet pause. Then, he closed the notebook slowly.

The park didn't offer solutions. That wasn't its purpose. However, it gave him room to see where he still defaulted to performing instead of leading, where he tightened his grip when trust would have been more effective. Where fear still had a seat at the table—even if it no longer ran the meeting.

His reflection was about owning mistakes rather than trying to fix flaws.

Before he stood, he traced the edge of the notebook spine with his thumb. Leadership was about learning while you walked, rather than learning how to arrive.

As he made his way back toward the building, one of the junior employees looked up, startled to recognize him. Their eyes met for half a second. She gave a slight nod, uncertain, but not uncomfortable.

Alex nodded back, quiet and steady. He kept walking.

LEADERSHIP COACHING ROUNDTABLE

The afternoon light spilled across the second-floor flex space. Loops of dry-erase ink still covered the whiteboard walls from a previous strategy session. Someone had arranged the chairs in a loose circle and left a half-eaten tray of snacks on the credenza. There were no laptops open, no screen waiting for a presentation. Just six people, a closed notebook, and a question written in black marker at the front of the room.

Leadership: What We're Still Learning

Alex sat forward in his chair, elbows resting on his knees, a pen in one hand. His notebook was on the table beside him. He glanced around the room—Lisa, Jordan, Mark, Alicia, Brent. Everyone was present but relaxed.

"I know we've been moving fast lately," he said. "Delivering. Solving problems. Getting things done."

He waited a beat before continuing. "Today isn't about deliverables. It's about the parts of leadership we don't usually name."

His eyes moved around the circle again. "We talk a lot about growth. Let's talk about where it's still happening. One question: What's one leadership blind spot you're working on right now?" He didn't call on anyone. He left space for someone to step in.

Lisa shifted slightly, arms crossed but steady. "Perfection," she said. "I double-check work I already trust. Rewrite things someone else has already finished. It slows us down. I know that. But it makes me feel like I'm protecting the outcome." She exhaled. "I'm learning to stop chasing flawless and focus on forward."

Jordan nodded. "I see that in myself, too. But for me, it shows up in delegation. I pass things off, then follow up too early. Or I check in sideways. Or I end up redoing part of it."

He spun his pen once between his fingers. "It's not about control. It's about wanting the result to reflect well on the team. But I'm learning that trusting someone means letting them finish without me hovering."

He glanced toward Lisa. "Perfection's close relative might be pacing. I trust fast—but I let go slowly."

Lisa gave a faint smile. "Same tree."

Mark sat still for a moment before speaking. "Mine is speaking up. Especially when I disagree with someone more senior."

Everyone looked toward him. "I was taught early on that challenging authority puts a target on your back. So, I hold back—even when I know I should speak." He didn't elaborate.

Brent leaned forward, elbows on knees. "I think mine is assuming people won't listen, so I don't bother saying much unless I'm 100% sure. That's how it was at Summitpoint—speak up and get shut down, or worse, assigned the fallout."

He paused. "Here, that's not the vibe. Still feels weird not bracing for it, though."

Alex nodded slightly, letting that land without trying to fix it.

He rested his pen on his knee. "I still catch myself trying to prove I belong."

The group was quiet, waiting. "Even now. Even here. I have the title and the team. But if something goes sideways, my first instinct is to fix it fast and move on. That's not trust. It feels more like a performance."

He looked at the others. "I want to lead from clarity, not fear of being seen as unprepared."

Alicia glanced at the whiteboard, then down again. Her voice was low, a little stiff. "For me, it's control." She didn't explain. But the room waited.

"I like knowing where the lines are. Who owns what. When that's blurry, I get tense. And I know that can come off like I'm shutting people down."

She looked at no one in particular. "I don't think it's about trust but about what happens when you've learned not to expect it."

A quiet acknowledgment passed through the group—nothing loud, but enough to matter.

Alex looked at the marker in his hand, then stood and walked to the whiteboard. He wrote three words beneath the heading.

SEEN. STRETCHED. SUPPORTED.

He turned back to the group. "That's what I want us to be for each other."

No one clapped or added anything. The room stayed quiet—the kind that holds something steady. Eventually, the group stood. Some spoke in low voices. They walked out carrying the same workloads—but a little less weight.

WHERE LEADERSHIP QUIETLY GROWS

The west-side break room was quiet in that late-hour kind of way—ambient light from the corner windows stretched long across the floor, cutting through the soft glow from overhead. The usual clatter of cups and the hum of the fridge filled the space with just enough sound to keep it from feeling empty.

Alex stood at the machine, jacket still on, sleeves rolled once. His stance was relaxed, grounded, but present. He wasn't feeling worn down—he was processing. The kind of stillness that follows after momentum.

Casey stepped in, espresso in hand, tablet tucked under her arm. She glanced toward him with a half-smile.

Alex raised an eyebrow as she crossed the room. "Why do you still come way down here for coffee? I'm sure the executive floor has something fancier."

Casey smirked. "It does. But the coffee up there tastes like strategy. This one tastes like culture."

He chuckled, grabbed a second mug from the rack, and handed it to her without asking. The rhythm was familiar now—no pretense or performance.

They moved to the window-side nook, where two chairs sat angled toward each other. Alex sat with ease, but open. The kind of posture that says, "I'm not in a hurry, and I'm not hiding."

He glanced out the window before he spoke. "That round-table earlier—it hit harder than I expected."

Casey set her espresso down and waited. She didn't need to prompt him. He continued.

"People showed up with real things. Mark admitted he hesitates to speak. Lisa's letting go of perfection. Even Brent said he assumes no one's listening. And Alicia..." He paused. "She didn't open up fully, but she didn't shut down either."

He shifted slightly. "I told them I still try to prove I belong."

Casey studied him for a moment. "Do you think you still need to?"

Alex didn't flinch. "Not as often. But it's still there. That reflex to solve everything. To look prepared. Like leadership is something you earn by hiding uncertainty."

Casey leaned forward slightly, elbows on her knees. "And what's that costing you?"

Alex exhaled—not in defeat, but in honesty. "Presence. Trust. Maybe even space for others to rise."

She nodded slowly. "So—what's the shift you're leaning into?"

He turned back toward the window, watching a few employees cut across the courtyard, hands tucked in their pockets against the wind. "Letting go of being the answer. Leading in a way that multiplies—not manages—capability."

His voice held a calm resolve. "I want the people around me to know they're trusted—without needing to earn it again every day."

Casey tilted her head. "That's not a performance metric."

He met her gaze. "No. It's a practice."

She smiled faintly. "And a hard one to measure."

"Which makes it the most important one," Alex said.

They sat for another minute. Two leaders, both still learning, both still leading. The kind of silence that invited presence instead of noise.

When Casey finally stood, she gave him a slight nod, took her espresso, and walked out without fanfare.

Alex stayed.

He looked down at the mug between his hands, then toward the empty chair across from him.

For a long time, I chased control because it made me feel safe. Now I see that safety was in being known—and letting others be known, too.

He stood slowly and headed back toward the floor. The coffee stayed unfinished, but the clarity lingered.

Culture Check with the Team

Mid-morning sunlight stretched across the conference room table in long, angled stripes. Scribbled notes, half-drunk coffee cups, and client decks dotted the surface—nothing polished, but everything active. No one waited for Alex to begin.

Lisa was already reviewing territory numbers on the whiteboard when Jordan walked in, tapping it twice with the back of his hand. "That Midwest conversion rate? You called it. I dug in last night. It's not the pitch. It's the follow-up timing."

"Then we adjust it," Lisa replied, already jotting an idea beneath her chart. "Push the recap within two hours, not 24."

Brent slipped in next, flipping open his notebook. "East Coast is lagging on B2 renewals. We're not losing the accounts, but we're not re-engaging early enough."

Mark, seated across the table, pulled up a tab on his tablet. "I can build a trigger based on contract age and past response time. Might automate the first touch."

Alicia, arms crossed, eyes sharp, spoke without fanfare. "If we're touching sooner, let's clean up the messaging. One strong line, not six paragraphs."

The team didn't pause to defend or posture—they just layered ideas. Adjusted. Aligned. It was the sound of a team that had stopped waiting for top-down direction and started leading where they stood.

Alex leaned forward, pen in hand, but no notes yet written. "What else?" he asked, but it wasn't a prompt. It was an opening.

Lisa didn't flinch. "We're over-compensating on the pitch with some newer reps. I've been stepping in too fast instead of letting them work through the reps."

Jordan shrugged. "Same here. I jump in during calls too early. Trying to rescue the close instead of letting them learn the rhythm."

Brent tapped his pen against the table. "I used to push numbers harder. Now, I'm asking more questions. I think it's landing better, but it still feels slow."

Mark chimed in. "I've been tracking my own responses—making sure I'm not the guy who only speaks when there's a problem."

All eyes shifted to Alicia. She hesitated, then said, "I've always been sharp. But I'm working on being clear without cutting people down." Her voice was quieter, but not unsure. Culture matters more than cadence.

Alex finally added, "I'm still learning to coach in real time without making it about performance. Just about progress."

The room held the silence for a moment—nothing heavy, just shared weight.

He rose and wrote three words on the board.

SEEN. TRUSTED. ACCOUNTABLE.

Then, he looked around the table. "That's the culture we protect. Because if we don't own it, someone else will reshape it."

No one in the room clapped—and they didn't need to. They stood and filtered out in twos and threes—talking, teasing, checking calendars.

Alex stayed behind as the door clicked shut. He glanced at the words he'd written, then out the window to where the day had stretched into full motion.

At this point in previous meetings, Alex would have recapped the numbers, re-clarified the strategy, and reminded the team of the mission. But they didn't need that now. They weren't following his playbook. They were writing their own—and it still carried his fingerprints.

He uncapped his pen and added one more word beneath the others.

SHARED.

Then, he closed his notebook and stepped out to rejoin the floor.

THE MIRROR AND THE COMPASS

Early evening pushed long shadows across the carpet, stretching under the desk and catching the edge of file boxes stacked near the wall. Alex's office no longer looked curated. It looked lived in. Dog-eared paperbacks lined the uneven shelves. A Summitpoint report, scribbled with margin notes, rested near a thank-you card pinned to the lamp. On the whiteboard, a streak of dry-erase marker cut across a to-do list that had been left unfinished.

He sat at his desk, posture upright but unguarded, his laptop open in front of him. He was excited about meeting with his leadership coach, Lucas. Alex was initially concerned about hiring a coach since he thought there wasn't value in it. Even though things were going well, Alex saw significant progress in his personal and professional life. This was a time to focus on the future and being goal-oriented.

Alex had started the session by describing the team's momentum—how Brent was initiating follow-ups without being asked, how Alicia was contributing with less edge and greater clarity, and how Lisa had begun coaching new reps without overstepping. He recounted the roundtable, the culture check, even a few moments he'd caught in passing. Then, he paused.

He turned slightly, pen in hand, and glanced at the notepad on the desk beside him. A few lines captured the reflection that had cracked something open.

Self-awareness builds confidence.
Strengths are the key.
Celebrate your team's wins—and your own.
Reproduce your mindset in others.

Lucas hadn't told him what to do. He never did. He asked the kind of questions that held up a mirror and quietly waited for Alex to name what he saw.

Lucas asked, "Where are you in the momentum?"

"I'm present," Alex had said slowly, "but sometimes, I'm still waiting for someone to tap me on the shoulder and say I've done enough."

Lucas leaned in slightly. "What would 'enough' look like if you stopped trying to prove and started trusting?"

Now, alone in the quiet, Alex replayed that question. He turned toward the whiteboard, cleared a fresh space in the top corner, and started writing.

CELEBRATE EFFORT, NOT JUST RESULTS.

MODEL VULNERABILITY BEFORE ASKING FOR IT.

DEFINE "ENOUGH" BEFORE THE PRESSURE DEFINES IT FOR YOU.

LEADERSHIP IS A MINDSET I CAN SCALE.

Lucas had helped him spot a blind spot: the tendency to lead through responsiveness rather than intention. Always reacting and catching the next thing, but rarely pausing long enough to recognize when the work of influence had already begun.

He stared at the board, then added one final note—larger than the rest.

MY JOB IS NO LONGER TO BE THE MAP. IT'S TO BE A COMPASS TO GUIDE THEM ON THE PATH.

Out in the hallway, the late-day energy hummed—Jordan talking to someone about a new lead strategy, Lisa and Alicia sketching something on a notepad, Brent crossing the floor to double-check a data pull before tomorrow's pitch.

They weren't waiting for him. They were building what he'd hoped for—and more.

Alex stepped into the doorway, watching for a moment. He didn't need to redirect or reframe. He'd already done that work. What mattered now was nurturing the culture that was emerging.

He grabbed his bag from the wall hook, left the laptop open, and let the lights stay on behind him.

As he stepped out onto the floor, the team moved around him, not under him or behind him, but beside him.

THE COMPASS IN HIS POCKET

The building had emptied, leaving only the low hum of lights and the occasional clack of a closing door. Alex lingered at the edge of the open floor, watching as the last of the team wrapped up their day. There was no grand exit or final announcement. Just people packing up, nodding their goodbyes, and heading home with the quiet satisfaction of a job well done.

Alex returned to his office momentarily to gather something he had nearly forgotten—an envelope with an old compass that had sat in his drawer since Casey gave it to him a while back.

He turned it over in his hand, thumb grazing the edge.

Relational strength. *That one had come slowly—learning to lead without needing the credit, making space for others to rise.*

Authentic presence. *He hadn't always gotten that right, but recently, he'd stopped performing and started showing up whole.*

Purposeful resilience. *He had earned that through breakdowns, resistance, and reflection.*

Growth through challenges. *Every detour had pointed him forward, not backward.*

He tucked it into his bag. He planned to pass it on when the time felt right, when the next leader needed a quiet reminder of their direction.

REFLECT

1. What beliefs about leadership did you once hold that no longer serve the team, or you?
2. When have you led from insecurity rather than intention? How do you respond when someone tests your trust?
3. What part of your leadership feels most like performance? Why? Who do you lead best—and who might you unintentionally overlook?
4. Do you create space for others to contribute, or simply manage outcomes?
5. What feedback have you quietly ignored that might hold truth?
6. When was the last time you celebrated your growth? Why did you wait?

ACTION

1. What's one mindset you need to reproduce in the leaders around you this quarter?
2. How will you reinforce strengths-based feedback in the next team meeting?

3. How can you visibly model vulnerability without diminishing confidence?
4. What are you doing to ensure psychological safety during one-on-one meetings?
5. Where can you hand over leadership in a way that builds someone else's voice?
6. How can you create a cultural moment that reinforces our values this week?

To Alex,

Power isn't what you hold–it's what you're trusted to give away.

From, Casey

CHAPTER 11

LESSONS FROM THE COMPASS

Resilience is not about bouncing back. It's about moving forward."

-Adam Grant

The rooftop hadn't caught the full weight of the day yet. Sunlight filtered through spring blooms, laying soft shadows across damp stone. The scent of mint and soil lingered in the stillness—a steady and unhurried space that arrived before the day.

Alex set two coffees on the bench and opened his notebook, flipping through a few marked-up pages. The city murmured below—delivery trucks, bikes, a hiss of brakes—but up here, none of it pressed in.

Lisa stepped onto the roof and made her way over without a word. Her walk was different now—steady, unhurried. Something in her posture had settled.

"You always beat me here," she said, sitting beside him.

"Only on days ending in 'y.'"

She smirked and took her coffee. Silence stretched between them. It felt comfortable and familiar. No one scheduled these check-ins—they happened naturally, right when needed.

"Reflecting or troubleshooting?" she asked, eyes on the skyline.

"Neither," Alex replied. "Just noticing."

They sat with it for a while. Lisa turned. "What are you noticing?"

"That you've stopped leading from urgency," he said. "You used to move like something was chasing you. Now? Like you're choosing where to go."

Lisa gave a quiet laugh. "Remember that onboarding week when I copied Howard's tone word-for-word? Thought sounding confident meant being cold."

Alex nodded, remembering. Back then, he would've corrected her. Now, he just listened, which said more about his growth than anything in his notebook.

He flipped to a fresh page and turned the notebook toward her.

Relational Strength.

Authentic Presence.

Purposeful Resilience.

Growth Through Challenges.

Lisa read each line slowly, fingers brushing under the second one. "That one took the longest."

"Same," Alex said, voice lower now.

She leaned back, eyes closed for a moment in the warm light. "Funny how we think leadership's about certainty," she said. "Turns out, it's just the opposite."

"Certainty is easy," he said. "Growth takes more effort."

Lisa reached for the pen, turned the notebook back toward her, and added one word beneath the list.

Trust.

No explanation. Just the truth. Alex looked at her, steady and still. She didn't need answers anymore—just space.

RELATIONAL STRENGTH: PEOPLE FIRST, ALWAYS

The afternoon sun stretched long across the Horizon Valley floor, slanting in through the west-facing windows and catching the soft edges of desks and monitor arms. The office hummed with steady energy—conversations flowed smoothly without tension, and footsteps moved without urgency. There was momentum without pressure.

Alex moved quietly through the space, scanning for a quick opportunity to check in. He caught sight of Mel, one of the junior staffers, sitting a little hunched at her desk, half-turned toward her monitor but not typing. Her hand hovered above the mouse, motionless. Something in her posture told him this wasn't a moment of concentration. It was something else.

He crossed the aisle casually and leaned just enough against the edge of her desk to break the moment without startling it. "That report finished writing itself yet?" he asked gently.

Mel looked up, caught off guard by the presence but not by the tone. "Not even close," she admitted, her voice thinner than usual. "I've reworked the intro multiple times and still can't make it sound right."

Alex didn't glance at her screen. Instead, he pulled a nearby chair and sat beside her, not across, not above, just close enough to level the space between them.

"Want to talk it through?" he asked.

Mel hesitated, then nodded. "It's not just the report. I think I'm second-guessing everything this week. I keep wondering if I'm actually getting this—like, if I'm contributing, or if I'm just trying not to mess things up."

Alex let that land without filling it. Then, he said, "You're not the only one who's felt that."

Mel offered a faint smile. "I know everyone says that, but..."

Alex nodded. "I don't mean in theory. I mean here. I've sat where you are and had that exact thought. So has Lisa. Mark's just quieter about it. But trust me—he's had days where he wasn't sure his part mattered."

Mel's shoulders relaxed a bit, but her eyes stayed uncertain.

"You know what helped?" Alex continued. "When someone reminded me that the value of your work doesn't always show up as applause. Sometimes, it shows up as a teammate being able to move because you did your part well. It shows up when Lisa leads without a script now. Or when Brent builds a client relationship with zero tension. Those things didn't start with brilliance. They started with belief."

Mel took a deeper breath. "I think I forgot to look at it that way."

"That's okay," Alex said. "Joy gets buried when we're measuring ourselves by perfection. What if 'getting it right' just means learning and adjusting in real time? Because that's what all of us are still doing."

Across the floor, Lisa stood with two new hires, with a whiteboard marker in hand, listening intently instead of teaching. Brent walked by moments later and passed a note to Alicia, who nodded without hesitation. Everyone was working, but no one seemed to be trying to survive the day. They were in it together.

Alex gestured toward the wider team. "You see that? This culture—we're building it and protecting it. You're part of that build. And you don't have to be loud to shape it. Just honest and present."

Mel finally smiled—small but full. "I needed that," she said.

"I know," Alex replied. "We all do sometimes. And when you're ready, Lisa's going to want to see your draft. She trusts you."

Mel turned back to her screen. The cursor blinked, patient and steady.

Alex stood and gave the back of her chair a light tap. "I'll check in later. Write like you believe in what you're saying."

She nodded, her posture a little straighter, and her hands moved back into motion.

Alex stepped away, but not without noticing how the space had shifted—just slightly, but meaningfully. Mel wasn't the only one re-centered. That kind of leadership didn't start with him anymore. It was multiplying.

This is what leadership looks like when it is shared—when people don't just carry the compass but become it.

AUTHENTIC PRESENCE: LEADING WITHOUT PRETENDING

The breakout room sat tucked behind the main corridor. A whiteboard stretched across one wall, still scribbled with strategy notes from a previous sprint. The mounted screen cycled silently through checkpoint data. A team member had left the folders half-open at the center table, tucking pens into spiral bindings as if pausing a thought mid-sentence.

The team gathered slowly—Lisa, Brent, Alicia, and Mark settling into their usual rhythm. Alex walked in last, a tablet in one hand and a notepad under his arm. He didn't sit at the head of the table. He sat beside Alicia, setting his things down without a word.

He looked around the group momentarily as if to say they had his full attention.

"I want to shift gears," Alex said. "This isn't about timelines or metrics today. It's about maturity—and something that doesn't get talked about enough in leadership circles: authentic presence."

He glanced toward the whiteboard but didn't get up. "We spend a lot of time talking about what we do, how we do it. But not enough about who we're becoming as we lead."

The team was listening, still and open.

"Authentic presence," Alex continued, "isn't about being polished or about image. It's about being emotionally grounded enough to stop pretending. Leadership maturity is when you can act like yourself—without shrinking, inflating, or covering."

He looked toward Lisa, who met his gaze and nodded. Lisa stood then, stepping beside the whiteboard, marker uncapped but still idle in her hand.

"I've got something to own up to," she said. "Last month's sales initiative—I treated it like a checklist instead of a conversation."

She didn't rush her words. "I pushed hard. The numbers worked. But I bulldozed through tone and team input to get there. It got done, but it didn't feel right."

Brent leaned forward, arms crossed but open. "You're talking about the onboarding scripts?"

Lisa nodded. "Exactly. I tightened the language but didn't ask if it still sounded like us. I was more focused on 'professional' than personal. I thought that would signal capability."

Mark looked up from his notes. "I didn't push back, but I felt the drift. It was like polished at the cost of being real."

Alex added gently, "There's a version of leadership that says, 'Don't show doubt. Don't show the edges.' But what if that's exactly what makes people trust us?"

The room remained quiet for a moment, filled with a shared reflection among the team.

Alicia, quiet up to now, finally spoke. "I kept editing myself. In drafts. In meetings. I was trying to sound like what I thought you wanted, not what I actually meant."

Lisa turned toward her. "I didn't want that. But I see how I created it."

Alex looked across the table. "This is the shift. Leadership isn't about perfect messaging. It's about being mature enough to lead as yourself—and making space for others to do the same."

Lisa finally lifted the marker and wrote across the board in clean print.

Authentic Presence = Leading Without Pretending

She turned to the group. “This is where I want to lead from. Starting today.”

The others nodded. The meeting did not solve everything, but it had named what mattered.

As the team gathered their things and filtered out, Lisa stayed behind again, wiping the board slowly. Mark paused at the door.

“You used to lead like you had to prove something,” he said.

“I did,” Lisa replied. “But now? I just want to lead like I believe something.”

Mark didn’t say anything more. He didn’t need to.

Alex watched her from the hallway as she capped the marker and stood back, arms loose at her sides. There was no tension left in her posture.

Alex realized he was witnessing authentic leadership—the kind that emerged not from playing a part, but from being the person you’ve grown into. That presence made space for others to do the same.

PURPOSEFUL RESILIENCE: STAYING GROUNDED WHEN IT'S HARD

The project bay buzzed with late-morning energy—emails clicked out, whiteboards were updated, and team members slid between desks with coffee and questions. The week had been full but not frantic. Horizon Valley had hit its rhythm.

Lisa crouched beside a junior team member's desk in the far corner of the floor. Caleb, one of the newest hires, stared wide-eyed at his screen. A row of flagged emails filled the bottom of the screen, each replying to a client report he had accidentally sent without the final attachments. A small mistake, but it hit fast. The client was understanding, but Caleb wasn't.

Lisa rested a hand on the back of his chair. "Hey," she said, her voice quiet. "Breathe. You're okay."

Caleb's voice was tight. "I should've double-checked. I knew it wasn't final, but I thought—" He stopped. His hands stayed frozen over the keyboard.

Alex approached, having heard bits of the exchange from across the room. He stood behind Lisa momentarily before stepping closer, placing a fresh cup of tea beside Caleb's keyboard.

"No one's fired," Alex said with calm finality. "And no one's disappointed. Let's talk about what happens next."

Caleb blinked. "Aren't you upset?"

Alex shook his head. "We don't lead with fear around here. Mistakes don't derail us—they realign us."

Lisa leaned in gently. "Say more about what you are feeling."

Caleb nodded. "A little embarrassed and anxious. Mostly—like I let everyone down."

Lisa nodded back. "Okay. I've been there. So has Alex. Probably every person on this floor."

She turned her chair to face him directly. "But here's what we've learned: You can't lead or grow from fear. That's not how we operate anymore. We come back to joy—because that's where real resilience lives."

Caleb looked between them, unsure whether to believe it. "Joy?"

Alex smiled. "Joy is about remembering that mistakes don't define you—and that your worth doesn't shift just because a task did."

He crouched next to the desk now, eye-level. "The real strength isn't in never messing up. It's in how you reset, reframe, and keep contributing with your head up."

Lisa tapped the desk softly. "So, how do we do that right now? First step?"

Caleb took a breath. "Resend the right file?"

"Good," Alex said. "Second step?"

A slight pause. "Follow up with a clear message. Own the mistake?"

Lisa nodded. "Perfect. And third?"

Caleb glanced up, a faint smile breaking through. "Don't spiral about it?"

Alex leaned back, his expression easing. "That's the one."

As Caleb got to work, Lisa turned toward Alex, her voice low. "He reminds me of me, a few years ago."

Alex nodded. "Me, too. Back then, I thought resilience meant powering through. Now, I know—it's about returning to joy when fear tries to steal it."

They stood together for a beat, watching as Caleb's shoulders relaxed. The team didn't erase the mistake, but they shared its weight—and that made all the difference. The tension lifted.

Alex knew mature leadership didn't mean pretending mistakes didn't happen. It meant making sure no one had to walk through them alone—and reminding them that joy was still an option.

GROWTH THROUGH CHALLENGES: PROGRESS OF MATURITY

Horizon Valley's shared kitchen glowed in the soft light of early evening. The sun angled low across the tile floor, catching the edges of the cabinetry and the curve of two coffee mugs left near the sink. Voices filtered faintly from the lobby, but the space itself felt like an exhale, a pause in a long day, not the end of one.

Mark sat at the tall counter with his laptop open, a system tracker printout fanned beside it. His pen moved slowly and steadily. He wasn't racing the clock. It was the kind of task that didn't earn praise but prevented panic.

Alex stepped into the room, grabbed a mug from the drying rack, and filled it with water. He noticed Mark immediately.

"Didn't expect to find you still grinding," Alex said, voice relaxed.

Mark didn't look up. "Cross-department update. I could wait, but tomorrow someone will open the wrong version and it'll turn into a fire drill."

Alex smirked and nodded. "Preventative leadership—quiet heroism."

Mark finally glanced up, his expression as even as his work. “It’s not the loud stuff that holds a team together. It’s the small, unseen fixes.”

Alex pulled out the chair across from him. “Exactly. The things no one claps for, but everyone relies on.”

They sat in easy silence for a moment. Their exchange wasn’t crisis management. It was maturity in motion.

“You’ve been especially quiet this week,” Alex added.

Mark rolled his pen between his fingers. “I’ve been watching. Noticing how we’re growing as a team. A few months ago, every hiccup felt like a derailment. Now? We adjust.”

He paused, eyes settling on the corner of his printout. “It made me realize—I used to default to staying out of the way. Do the work, avoid the spotlight. But I’ve started asking myself, is that leadership or just a habit I picked up during the Howard years?”

Alex leaned forward, elbows resting lightly on the counter. “A lot of managers lead like that—performing to avoid critique. They look composed, but it’s really just emotional avoidance.”

Mark nodded slowly. “I’ve seen that, yeah. The ones who treat every challenge like a crisis. I call them ‘Crisis Kings.’ They don’t lead through difficulty—they panic in it. And everyone else ends up managing their emotions instead of the problem.”

Alex’s eyes narrowed slightly in agreement. “Fear stalls growth. Always has. But people start to feel safe again when a leader carries joy—even in the hard stuff. This creates community. Our strengths grow in relationship to others- not alone.”

Mark pulled a folded page from his folder—a messy sketch of the team’s original workflow, now marked with red arrows, notes, and a reimagined structure.

“This,” he said, sliding it across the counter. “That was six months ago. It nearly cracked us.”

Alex studied the paper. “And now?”

Mark tapped the new sketch. “Now, we adapt. We keep each other moving forward.”

Alex looked at him, proud but steady. "You know what I see? Maturity. Because the pressure doesn't shape you anymore. You shape it."

Mark smiled faintly. "Have you ever thought that maybe maturity isn't about becoming unshakable? It's about choosing not to disappear when things are hard."

Alex exhaled. "Exactly. Most people get promoted because they deliver results. But it is shallow and short-lived. But the best leaders I know? They grow people."

He reached for his mug, then paused, looking at Mark. "Thanks for holding the line. The team doesn't always see it—but I do."

The moment didn't need more. Two leaders practiced leadership in that room—quietly, with strength, no longer leading as if everything were an emergency.

COACHING SESSION: SPACE TO SEE

The screen blinked once, then settled into the quiet rhythm of their usual calls. Alex sat centered, back straight, a notepad nearby but untouched. Lucas's window came into view—still, simple, calm. His presence had a way of lowering the volume of everything else. Neither of them rushed to speak.

Lucas offered the first words, not a question about work or leadership. "How are you showing up today?"

Alex considered that. "Present, mostly. A little tight around the edges."

Lucas nodded slowly. "What do you mean 'tight around the edges?'"

Alex's eyes shifted inward. "I think I'm carrying more than I meant to." Alex tapped the side of his pen. "There's a performance review coming. Howard. And I can already feel the old muscle memory trying to kick in."

Lucas didn't move to solve. His tone didn't change. "Who do you want to be?"

Alex didn't answer quickly. "More clear. Less reactive. I'm learning not to lead from fear, but from who I actually am."

Lucas gave a single, steady nod. "And what helps you be who you actually are?"

Alex glanced down, then back up. "Quiet moments. Space like this. And watching my team step into their strength—it reminds me I don't have to carry everything."

He paused. "I used to think leadership meant proving I belonged. Lately, I think it means showing others they already do."

Lucas sat with that. "What would it look like to lead from that place in your next conversation?"

Alex let the question settle, and then he wrote something in his notebook. They were simple and honest words.

I don't have to defend my growth. I can embody it.

He looked back at the screen. "I'm ready to stop rehearsing the version of me he might approve of."

Alex stopped, letting the weight fall away.

VALUED OR VALUABLE

Howard's office was quiet, cold, and calculated. It always felt more like a display of awards and company accolades than a workspace. Nothing out of place. Nothing personal. Just glass and angles and the low hum of a clock ticking on a wall that had never known laughter.

Alex sat across from the desk, shoulders back and alert. He knew what this was. The review in front of Howard was just a prop. This meeting wasn't about performance but about power.

Howard flipped through the last few pages of the report, his fingers too slow to be casual. "Operations have stabilized. Client metrics are clean. You've kept your division in check."

He looked up, voice flat. "But from here on out, I'll be taking a more hands-on approach. Reviewing your approvals. Sitting in on key syncs. I want to ensure things stay on track."

Alex blinked once. That was the setup—a disguised demotion without a title change. Howard was boxing him in.

"So... micromanagement?" he asked evenly.

Howard gave a clipped shrug. "Call it what you want. I call it leadership."

A slow, quiet realization sank into Alex's chest—not sharp, just heavy. The kind of weight that felt like confirmation. He'd been waiting for this moment without knowing it.

For a long time, Alex had been chasing something here. He wasn't thinking about a promotion or a title, but simple recognition. A signal that his way of leading, through people, with people, was seen as valuable. That maybe he mattered beyond the numbers he delivered.

He sat forward slightly. "Am I valued here, Howard? Or just useful in making your own little kingdom?"

Howard didn't flinch. "You've produced results."

"That's not what I asked." Alex responded.

The silence between them became tense. Howard's face remained unreadable.

Alex continued, slower now, more grounded. "I'm the only division lead still here from before the merger. The only one who stayed when it got hard. And I didn't stay to be controlled—I stayed to build something worth trusting."

Howard's eyes narrowed. "You're too relational. You let people take up too much space."

Alex didn't break eye contact. "I want people to own their work, not fear me. If that's a problem, then maybe we're not talking about leadership but about obedience."

Howard leaned back, folding his arms. "People need strict direction."

"They need belief," Alex said. "And not just in the vision of the company. In themselves. That's how growth happens."

Howard gave a dismissive tilt of his head. "You've gotten soft."

"No," Alex replied calmly. "I've gotten clear."

The room fell quiet again. Alex didn't rush to fill it. He looked down for a moment, then back at Howard.

"You've spent years trying to fix me, but I don't think you've ever tried to know me. Do you even know what my strengths are—who I am beyond producing results?"

Howard shifted in his seat. "I know you're competent."

"Competency is not a strength," Alex said. "What made you want to hire me?"

The words had weight now. Alex wasn't lashing out but letting go.

"You remove the relationship from everything. You act like people are interchangeable. And I used to think if I just worked hard enough, you'd finally see me." Alex paused, just for a breath. "But I don't need that anymore."

Howard said nothing.

Alex stood slowly. "You don't even care to know my strengths. But I do. And so does my team. That's enough."

He turned toward the door, pausing only once more.

"For what it's worth," he said quietly, "I hope someday you stop making people feel like they have to earn your approval. Because that's not leadership. It's insecurity in disguise."

And then, he walked out.

In the hallway, Alex felt his hands settle at his sides, steady. For the first time in a long time, he hadn't tried to win the moment. He'd just shown up as himself—no defensiveness or disguise.

And maybe that was the real win: not convincing Howard but no longer needing to. Leading with strength wasn't about holding control but releasing the need to be seen by someone who refused to look.

RECALIBRATION

Alex closed the door to his office with a soft click and leaned against it for a moment, letting the silence settle. No one had followed. No one had seen.

He wasn't rehearsing a response or planning a repair for the first time in a long while. He was just sitting in it—the aftermath of truth.

He stared at the review still in his hands, the one Howard had slid across the desk like a prize. It read well—substantial numbers, positive feedback, a neat performance summary—but it was hollow. The report measured everything trackable and ignored everything that mattered.

He laid it down. Then, he opened his notebook and didn't write. Not right away. He let his thoughts surface on their own.

What do I want now? I'm not looking for permission or approval. Not even to be tolerated for my methods. I want to lead freely with vision and with people who want to grow, not just produce.

He leaned back in his chair, his eyes drifting to the ceiling. The past few years have been about weathering the storm—learning to stay steady in someone else's chaos, creating clarity when leadership only offered control, and being a leader worth following when no one was modeling it.

He thought about his team—when Lisa challenged and collaborated, Mark spoke with more presence than words, Brent started asking questions not out of fear but out of ownership, and Alicia, still guarded, but leaning in.

And him? He wasn't chasing approval anymore. He was shaping culture. Quietly. Patiently. Powerfully.

He looked at the small compass sketch in the corner of his whiteboard. It reminded him of where he was going and how he would get there.

His pen finally moved. He wrote what came to mind.

Vision, not reaction.

Presence, not performance.

Build what outlasts you.

He closed the notebook and stared out the window. The city looked quiet from this floor, like something was waiting to begin.

Whatever happens next, I'm not shrinking again. Alex let the hour stretch, uninterrupted—just him, the page, and the future.

A FRIENDLY VISIT FROM AN OLD FOE

The office felt heavier than it had that morning. The blinds were half-drawn, muting the light into soft streaks across the floor. Alex sat at his desk, a file open in front of him but untouched. His fingers hovered over the keyboard, still processing what had happened upstairs.

He had stood up to Howard. Calmly, clearly, and without folding. And now, he didn't know if he'd just crossed the invisible line that got people replaced.

He leaned back in his chair, trying to slow the noise in his head. His breath caught for a second longer than usual. Part of him was proud. The other part? Bracing.

A knock at the door pulled him upright.

Trent Mallory stood in the doorway, his tie loose and collar open. His posture was casual, but his eyes were focused. The last time Alex saw him, Trent had been all urgency and edge, navigating the complexities of merger politics. Now, he looked like someone who had recently remembered how to exhale.

"Hey, Tiger, am I interrupting?" Trent asked.

Alex blinked, then motioned him in. "Not at all."

Trent stepped in and closed the door behind him. "Didn't plan on dropping by. Just decided to follow a hunch."

Alex raised an eyebrow. "You following your gut these days?"

Trent gave a short smile. "Trying to catch up to what's already happening."

He glanced around the room. "This place feels different. You feel different."

Alex didn't deny it. "We've done some unlearning."

Trent nodded, then pulled a folder from his satchel. No fanfare or buildup. He placed it on the desk and slid it forward.

"I haven't talked to anyone here. There's no backchanneling. This isn't about Horizon Valley. It's about you."

Alex didn't reach for the folder.

Trent continued. "I joined the board of a nonprofit just outside the city. Small team. Big heart. But they're early—still building structure, still learning how to lead without spinning their wheels."

Alex stayed quiet.

"They need someone who can build without ego," Trent said. "Someone who knows how to lead people—not just manage outcomes. And frankly, someone who's had to wrestle through that difference firsthand."

Alex finally glanced at the folder, then looked up again. "Just so we're clear—Lisa's not allowed to go anywhere."

Trent smirked. "Noted. I'll back away from your MVP. But I am interested in Howard's MVP. You."

Alex finally spoke. "Why me?"

"Because I've been watching," Trent said. " Just paying attention."

He rested his hands lightly on the edge of the desk. "The way you've shown up lately—especially under pressure. That's not the guy I met during the merger. You're leading like someone who doesn't need to prove anything. You're steady. And people follow that."

Alex glanced at the folder but didn't open it. "I just told Howard I wasn't going to lead by pretending anymore."

Trent nodded once. "Then maybe this is the right time."

Alex still didn't move.

Trent stepped back. "No pitch. No pressure. Just a door, if you want to look through it."

He left a card on the desk and turned toward the door. "I know you just came out of a hard meeting. I didn't mean to pile on."

Alex's voice stopped him. "You didn't. You reminded me that I still get to choose who I become."

Trent gave a slight, sincere nod. "Exactly."

He left without another word.

Alex stared at the folder for a long moment. He didn't open it right away. Instead, he rested his hand on top of it, grounding himself.

What came next was up to him.

THE COMPASS FORWARD

The café inside the Horizon Valley building was nearly closed for the night. Lights ran low across the floor, casting soft amber rings around the corners of each table. The hum of a dishwasher cycled faintly in the back. Two staffers chatted quietly near the counter, their voices too soft to follow. The rest of the space felt like a held breath.

Alex sat by the window, coffee cooling beside his hand. His notebook lay open, but the pen was untouched. He had been sitting there for a while, letting the quiet do its work.

Casey stepped in, thermos in hand. She spotted him immediately and made her way over without hesitation. She dropped into the seat across from him with the kind of familiarity that didn't need permission.

"You're usually on the roof this time of night," she said, settling her cup down. "What brought you to ground level?"

Alex didn't answer right away. He looked at the streetlight outside the window, watching its reflection slide across the rim of his mug. Then, Alex glanced at her. "An unexpected opportunity found me today," he said. "It came out of nowhere. And there's something about it that feels compelling."

Casey didn't react with surprise or concern. She simply nodded, then leaned in slightly. "What part of it draws you in?"

Alex shrugged. "It's not the role exactly. It's the space it might offer—to build something from the inside out. Slower, quieter. But more intentional."

She tilted her head. "What would you be leaving behind?"

He paused, eyes on the notebook before closing it gently. "A team that trusts each other. A culture we fought to restore. The kind of leadership I never imagined I'd get to be part of."

Casey let that sit for a beat before asking, "Is it possible to bring that same leadership with you? Or does it only live here?"

That question landed. Alex's fingers drifted to the notebook's inside cover, tracing the compass's small sketch. Just below the drawing were four words.

Relational. Authentic. Resilient. Growing.

"I don't think geography is a major factor," he said. "It's about remembering which direction I'm pointing to—especially when it gets dark."

Casey smiled, quietly but knowingly. "That's what leaders are. Not maps but compasses. We don't always give the route. We just help people find their north."

Outside the window, the streetlights blinked softly. Lisa passed through the lobby with a folder tucked under her arm. She paused when she saw them and gave a small wave through the glass. Alex raised his coffee in return. Just a flicker of connection—but it meant something.

Casey rose to leave, resting a hand on his shoulder briefly. "Whatever you decide, don't choose based on fear of losing what you've built. Choose based on who you've become while building it."

Alex looked up at her. "I heard there's an all-hands meeting in the morning. You know anything about it?"

She paused at the edge of the table, her smile a little mischievous. "There's an announcement."

"Good announcement?" Alex asked.

"Depends," she said. "But I'd get there early."

She walked toward the door without another word.

Alex stayed seated. He stared at the closed notebook, not weighed down by the weight of the last few years, the choices ahead. Positive thoughts about the people he now leads and trusts. There was no anxiety in him tonight—only clarity. And that felt like the real win.

The compass was never the destination. Just a reminder to keep pointing true. And tomorrow? Tomorrow would mark something new.

REFLECT

1. Are you creating space for others to lead—or just for them to follow?
2. What does emotional maturity look like in your leadership today?
3. Do you seek to understand or win in moments of conflict?
4. Do you believe you are valuable beyond the outcomes you produce?

5. What assumptions about leadership are you still unlearning?
6. Who is rising around you, and have you noticed?

ACTION

1. What's one small way you can model relational strength on your team this week?
2. How can you help someone return to joy after a difficult moment today?
3. Who on your team needs to be seen, not just evaluated?
4. Where can you pause before reacting and turn the moment into one of alignment?
5. What conversation do you need to finish, not to resolve conflict, but to restore trust?
6. How will you make space for someone else to lead in the next 30 days?

Alex,

Leaders are not maps but compass. We don't always give the route. We just help people find their north.

–Casey

CHAPTER 12

HORIZON VALLEY'S FUTURE

Every time you empower someone else to lead, you extend your legacy beyond yourself."

-Ryan Crittenden

The Horizon Valley auditorium pulsed with quiet anticipation. Employees from every department—Horizon Valley and Summitpoint alike—filled the tiered rows that wrapped around the wide stage. It looked like integration, but the subtle posture of the divide still lingered. Arms crossed. Faces guarded. Regardless, everyone sensed the shift coming.

Alex sat in the third row between Lisa and Brent, jacket off, coffee in hand, mind already putting the pieces together from the day before.

The lights dimmed. A spotlight clicked on. Casey walked out alongside the company's top leaders—Howard, Trent Mallory, and the rest. Though physically the smallest among them, her presence immediately eclipsed the others. She didn't break formation, didn't push ahead. But somehow, she still led the walk. Sleeves casually rolled, posture grounded, gaze steady. She didn't demand attention, but everyone's eyes were on her.

Xander Jay, Chairman of the Board, stepped to the podium and adjusted the mic.

"Thank you all for being here," he began, "This moment matters—for our future, and for everyone who believes leadership should evolve."

He offered a short, respectful nod to outgoing CEO David Chen, then leaned in.

"And now, with great confidence and anticipation for the future, I'm thrilled to announce the newest CEO of Horizon Valley, Casey Turner."

Applause broke out in bursts—scattered at first, then steadily building. Cameras flashed. The energy lifted like a held breath finally released.

Casey stepped forward. Howard clapped, but barely—just two polite taps. Eyes flat and face neutral. His silence spoke volumes more than any speech ever could.

Casey took the mic, calm and grounded. The room leaned in.

"Thank you, Xander. And thank you to all of you—onsite, remote, and watching from afar."

"Stepping into this role isn't about achievement. It's about stewardship. For me, leadership isn't being the smartest person in the room but seeing what others carry, and creating space for them to bring it fully."

A few heads in the crowd nodded slowly. Alex could tell that the people listening were absorbing every word.

"Legacy isn't what you leave behind. It's who you lift up while you're still here. The future of Horizon Valley won't be built on titles or org charts. It will be built by people anywhere in the company who lead with clarity, courage, and compassion."

"I'm here to build a culture where people are valued for their unique contributions and strengths—because that's where our real momentum begins."

Applause rose again, louder and full-bodied this time. Everyone stood. The shift had happened, and every person in that room knew it.

Alex didn't look at the stage. His gaze found Howard—still, upright, jaw flexed tight. There was still no applause or shift in expression. He was motionless—the man who had brought Alex to Horizon Valley but never invested in him as a leader. Howard built systems. Casey built people. And in this moment, everyone could see the difference.

Alex turned to the stage. Casey looked over at everyone in the room and smiled. She was glad to be with them all.

He leaned toward Lisa and said quietly, "That's how you build a legacy."

Lisa nodded slowly, eyes still forward. "And that's the kind people remember."

A Room That's No Longer His

Three months had passed since Casey stepped into the CEO role. Some things were changing fast, but others were slow and methodical. Horizon Valley's culture was becoming its second-biggest competitive advantage, only behind its people.

Morning light cut through half-drawn blinds, striping the floor in pale gold. The room sat untouched—blank notepad, cold coffee, tablet off. Quiet, not from peace, but from something fading. Trophies behind the desk still caught the light. Howard didn't. He stared at nothing, sitting in the space between what was and what no longer is.

A soft knock broke the stillness.

"Come in," Howard said, without turning.

Trent Mallory stepped inside, one hand in his pocket, coat still buttoned.

"Didn't mean to intrude," Trent said, tone neutral.

Howard shrugged. "You didn't. I'm not exactly busy anymore."

Trent crossed the room but didn't sit. "You know, I thought you might take a few weeks off. Recharge."

Howard gave a dry laugh. "For what? Another round of meetings I won't be leading? I'll probably die at this desk. Seems fitting."

Trent didn't smile. He stepped in closer, voice steady. "If you stay in that chair past your time, you're not showing dedication. You're blocking growth. You're hurting the leaders who come next."

Howard's jaw tightened. "I built Horizon Valley's revenue engine. I hired Alex. I gave him a runway. And now, he gets the applause while I get the door."

"You didn't give him a runway," Trent said. "You gave him rules. He had to find his own air."

Howard turned his head slightly, defensive heat rising. "He was unproven. Green. Every risk he took—he learned from watching me."

"No," Trent said, stepping in closer. "He learned despite you. You showed him control. Casey showed him purpose. That's the difference."

Howard scoffed. "So, now I'm the villain?"

"No," Trent said. "But you are the cautionary tale."

Silence hung thick between them. Howard's eyes flicked to the window, his reflection blurred by sunlight.

Trent took a breath. "Legacy isn't what you build. It's who you build. If you're not raising up leaders, you're not leaving one."

Howard looked away, bitterness quietly calcifying. "I gave everything to this place. And now, the future belongs to someone else."

"Because the future listens to who shows up with humility," Trent said. "And people are paying attention to how Alex leads. His team? They trust him. They're growing under him. And that didn't happen by accident."

Howard didn't respond. Just stared at the cold cup on his desk. His voice, when it came, was low and hollow. "I did everything for him."

"And what he needed," Trent said, " was a belief from a trusted leader."

Trent walked to the door, then paused. "The truth, Howard? Staying in the room doesn't make you relevant. Investing in people does." Then, he left.

Howard didn't move. The light shifted again, casting longer shadows across the shelves. The trophies still caught the glow, but none of it reached him.

They gave him the title for years. But no one followed him into the future.

SMALL SHIFTS, REAL CHANGE

Mid-afternoon light spilled across the collaboration hub, bouncing off glass walls and marked-up whiteboards. The space buzzed with quiet energy—clusters of conversation, laptops open, and actual work in motion.

At a high table, Alicia reviewed a shared screen with Brent. Her voice was steady, guiding rather than commanding.

"If we layer this with rollout data, what story are we missing?"

Mark leaned in the doorway, arms crossed. "Engagement didn't dip—it shifted platforms."

Brent clicked ahead. "Exactly. We weren't losing traction, just looking in the wrong place."

Mark stepped closer. "That chart used to rattle people. Now, you're pulling insight from it in minutes."

Alicia smiled. "People change when they're trusted."

Mark nodded. "Keep going."

Across the room, Jordan scrolled through a dashboard, headphones loose around his neck. A junior sales lead approached, hopeful.

"Could I run the process update next week? I've been shadowing—think I've got it."

Jordan didn't look up. "Stick to the script. It's more efficient."

"But Alicia said—"

"She's not running this. I am," Jordan cut in.

The junior lead stepped back, silenced. Jordan kept scrolling.

Mark watched quietly. "He's still playing defense," he said to Alicia. "Doesn't even see what he's holding back."

Alicia didn't look up. "He's choosing the safe route."

Mark nodded, eyes back on the room. Growth wasn't about knowing more, he realized—it was about being willing to become more.

SHIFTS IN THE ROOM

Casey looked up just as Howard stepped out of her office. He passed Alex and Lisa in the hallway—no words, just a nod. His expression was unreadable, but the energy was unmistakably final.

Casey didn't comment. She just gestured toward the table. "Come in."

Alex and Lisa stepped inside. No small talk. Lisa set her laptop down but didn't open it. Alex carried only a notebook.

"We've been looking at how to lean harder into team strengths," Alex said. "Let people do the work they're built to do."

Lisa nodded. "It's making a difference. Both in output and how people show up."

Casey gave a knowing smile. "That's the shift that matters."

She crossed to the whiteboard, uncapped a marker, and wrote two words.

LEADERSHIP LEGACY

Then, with the same calm tone, she added, "Howard submitted his retirement paperwork this morning—30 days."

Lisa blinked. "Just like that?"

Alex exhaled, not surprised. "Voluntary?"

Casey nodded once. "He did."

There was a pause, quiet, but not awkward. The kind that holds change without forcing anyone to fill it.

Casey returned to the table. "No press release. He built an engine, but the story moves forward without needing to relive every line."

Alex tapped his pen against the table. "That kind of ending says more than most speeches."

Lisa glanced over. "What now?"

Casey looked at her, steady. "Now, we lead from strength—not titles."

The three leaders spoke a little more, some as mentors to the learner, some as colleagues, and some as friends.

Casey smiled and thought about the two promising people in front of her.

Unspoken Expectations

Alex and Lisa made their way back to the sales bullpen. Lisa made a stop for coffee. The hallway outside the break room had gone still. Most of the building was dark, the glow of the vending machine reflecting off polished floors.

Lisa stepped out, notebook in hand, flipping a page as she walked. Focused. Unhurried.

"Hey," a voice said.

She turned. Jordan stood a few steps away, hands in his pockets. His face held something unresolved.

"Everything okay?" Lisa asked.

He shrugged. "Just thought we should talk."

She nodded toward the bench. "Sure."

They sat side by side. No tension. Just unfilled space.

Jordan spoke first. "You've been with Alex a lot lately."

Lisa didn't flinch. "We've been working through leadership transitions."

"Right." A beat. "It just feels like you got the stretch roles—the strategy. And I didn't."

Lisa looked forward. "I didn't ask for them. But I said yes when they came."

Jordan nodded slowly. "I figured we'd grow together. I kept my head down. Delivered. Thought that would be enough."

Lisa kept her voice even. "Leaders look for growth. I got in the trenches with Alex. I asked questions. Risked being wrong. That's where the trust started."

Jordan didn't respond right away. "I thought showing up meant getting it right."

"It means getting in it," she said.

He stared at the floor. "I missed it, didn't I?"

Lisa didn't soften. "Maybe. But missing it once doesn't mean you have to keep missing it. There's bound to be another chance around the corner."

Jordan stood, adjusting his bag. "Thanks for saying that."

Lisa watched him go. She knew the truth: Some people wait for permission. Others step in. Growth was never about who's first. It was about who's willing.

THE EXIT THAT ECHOED

The multi-purpose lounge had seen its share of potlucks and project launches. Today, the setup felt more formal. A foldable podium stood beside a modest refreshment table, featuring cut vegetables, finger sandwiches, and sugar-free brownies. The slideshow on the wall looped through a slow rotation of images.

Thank You, Howard

- Years of Results

The room was packed, but not warm. Conversations remained confined to tight, safe circles. Former direct reports lingered near the center, while Summitpoint employees stood back along the walls. It felt more like an obligation than a celebration.

Howard stood near the front, his hands folded behind him, his posture straight, his expression unreadable. He scanned the room, as if measuring the distance between presence and connection, and finding it wider than expected.

Alex stood with Lisa, Mark, and Casey near the back wall. They sipped coffee in silence.

Mark leaned in. "No cake?"

Lisa scanned the table. "Just sandwiches and regret."

Alex gave a small, dry smile. "You'd think someone would have more to say."

The slideshow rolled on: handshakes, sales charts, conference stages—Howard at the center of it all, always in control.

The mic stood empty. The mid-level manager who'd kicked off the event had already stepped down. There were a few polite claps. Some light nods. But no one moved. No one lined up. The room held an awkward pause.

Still, no one stepped forward.

Finally, Alex set his cup down and walked toward the podium. The silence thickened—not out of anticipation, but surprise.

He didn't speak for long.

"I wouldn't be at Horizon Valley if Howard hadn't brought me in," he said. "That decision changed the course of my career—and in many ways, how I see people and leadership. He challenged me to perform. To deliver. To show up under pressure."

He paused. "Not everything we learn from someone needs to be soft to be valuable. Some of it is grit. Some of it is clarity. Some of it... is the lesson of who we want to become, and what we don't want to miss along the way."

Alex turned toward Howard briefly. "I wish you the best in whatever comes next. And I mean that."

He stepped down without embellishment—just the truth.

Howard took the mic next. His words were brief and controlled.

"Thank you. It takes a long time to build something. I'm proud of what we achieved. Proud of the results we delivered. That's the legacy I leave behind."

He gave a short nod. No stories or warmth. Just punctuation.

The clapping was louder this time, but still polite. A few coworkers shook their hands out of routine. Their thanks were short. Metrics. Efficiency. Q4s.

From the back, Alex watched. He saw what had landed and what hadn't.

Howard built performance, but he forgot to develop people.

Alex stayed off to the side, watching as the room filled with people mingling and talking. Silently, he thought about Howard and his ending. And when the numbers fade, all that's left is how you made them feel. He turned and snuck out of the room.

THIS IS THE BEST THING FOR ME

The rooftop of Horizon Valley's main building caught the last of the day's light. The city stretched wide in every direction, washed in the soft amber of early evening. Far below, the hum of downtown buzzed faintly, distant enough to forget for a while. A few chairs sat scattered near the edges of the terrace, mostly unused. The air moved with a quiet chill, just enough to clear the mind.

Casey stepped out onto the rooftop and paused. Near the far railing, Alex stood alone. He was leaning forward slightly, his sleeves rolled up, and a coffee cup in one hand. The sunset framed him in silhouette, the glow cutting around his shoulders and softening the line of his posture.

“Knew I’d find you up here,” Casey said gently.

Alex didn’t turn. He just nodded, eyes still on the skyline.

“Needed a minute,” he said. “This place helps.”

She crossed the space slowly and joined him at the railing. They stood without speaking, the quiet between them holding steady and easily.

After a while, Alex broke the silence. “A couple of months ago, Trent Mallory approached me about being the executive director of a social impact nonprofit. We have been talking regularly about it. I’ve been thinking a lot about it lately.”

Casey looked at him, eyebrows raised slightly. She hadn’t expected the timing, but the news made sense. She knew that Alex had a bright future ahead of him.

“Oh yeah?” she asked, her voice warm. “What is holding you back?”

Alex gave a short and honest laugh, more breath than sound. “I don’t know. Feels like I hit a stride here.”

Casey turned to face him more fully. "Well, that is not a good enough reason to stay. You don't need my permission to stay or to go."

They stood in silence again. The breeze shifted. Below them, the city lights flicked on, one by one.

"I think I'm ready," Alex said. "This is the best thing for me."

Casey nodded slowly. "I agree."

Alex took a slow sip from his cup, then set it on the ledge beside him. "There's something else," he said. "I want to recommend Lisa to take over for me."

Casey didn't blink. "She's already on my shortlist."

"I trust her," Alex said.

Casey didn't hesitate. "That's harder to build."

Alex nodded. "She is going to do great. The team already knows and trusts her."

They both looked out again as the sun slipped below the horizon.

Casey silently agreed with Alex. She knew that leadership doesn't hand off like a baton. It passes like trust—quietly, between people who believe in each other more than they want control.

Passing the Compass

By early evening, the café had mainly cleared. A few laptops blinked sleepily in corners. The playlist hummed low and easy, the light golden against the windows. Horizon Valley was winding down.

Alex sat near the window, typing slowly, deliberately. His posture was relaxed, but there was a weight to it, as if something was closing in. The same table where he and Casey sat many times now held a different kind of conversation waiting to happen.

Lisa walked in with two coffees, spotted him, and crossed the room to him. She set one beside him. "Still working?" she asked.

"Tying up a few things," Alex said. "Almost done."

She took the seat across from him. They sipped quietly for a minute.

Then, Alex spoke, voice low. "I just wrote my letter of resignation."

Lisa's cup paused halfway to her mouth. "You're serious?"

He nodded. "It's time. Trent Mallory has offered me an executive director role at the non-profit he is on the board of."

"You're actually leaving," she said, eyes scanning his face.

Alex reached into his bag and pulled out a folder. "I wrote two letters today. One was my resignation. The other one is for you."

She opened it slowly. Typed lines, then handwritten notes—affirmation, encouragement, observations. Her name was at the top—a vote of confidence on paper.

"You've already been leading," Alex said. "This just makes it official."

Lisa held the folder, still taking it in. "You're really doing this."

"I wouldn't, if I thought the team wasn't ready." Alex answered.

Her eyes welled slightly, but she didn't blink it away. "You're not getting out of here that easily."

She pulled out her phone and sent a quick group text. Five minutes later, Mark, Jordan, Brent, and Alicia walked in, curious but unbothered. Lisa stood to greet them.

"He's leaving," she said. "Alex is moving on. He took a job at a non-profit with Trent Mallory."

The reactions were what you'd expect: shock, disbelief, a few muttered "no way" and "for real?" lines. Almost on cue, Mark cracked a joke about leaving when it's starting to get good. Someone laughed. Then, everyone did. The tension cracked. Casey walked by, unnoticed, and everyone was present with each other. She knew this was the best work she had ever done.

The team pushed the tables together. Someone grabbed napkins for tissues. They told stories—early mistakes, late-night pivots, inside jokes from the merger days. Brent teared up first. Alicia hugged him after. Even Jordan smiled—small, but unmistakably genuine.

One by one, they drifted out, each offering a hug or handshake. By the end, only Lisa and Alex remained.

She looked at him, eyes shining. “You built something here.”

“So did you,” he said. “You’re not holding it together. You’re leading it forward.”

He reached into his jacket and slid a small envelope across the table.

"Open it later," he said. "It's just a reminder of where you're pointing."

She didn't ask what it was. She just nodded.

When Lisa finally walked outside, the sky was dark and clear. Stars blinked quietly overhead. She opened the envelope by the streetlamp.

Inside was a small brass compass—simple, worn, steady—along with a folded note.

> *You don't have to know every step. You just have to help others find the direction. And Lisa, you already are.*

She closed her hand around it, then looked back up at the stars.

Leadership wasn't about having the answers. It was about becoming the kind of person others trusted to walk with them toward what's next. And tonight, she felt the weight of that—in the best way.

She walked on, the compass in her pocket. Quiet, steady, ready.

REFLECT

1. What values do you want people to remember when they think of your leadership?
2. Have you built something that can thrive without you? In what ways have you developed others to lead beyond you?
3. What unspoken culture have you contributed to in your organization?
4. Have you been more focused on recognition or reproduction?
5. What kind of stories will people tell about your leadership when you're not in the room?

ACTION

1. Who are you currently mentoring to lead?
2. How can you empower someone this week to stretch into their potential?
3. What practices can you start to make leadership more relational and values-based?
4. What can you do right now to make space for the next generation of leadership?

Dear Alex,

Leadership isn't being the smartest person in the room but seeing what others carry, and creating space for them to bring it fully.

Always, Casey

EPILOGUE

FULL CIRCLE

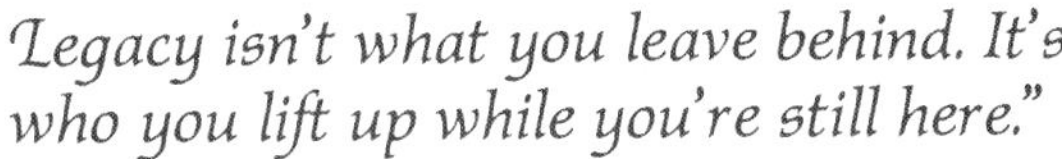

"Legacy isn't what you leave behind. It's who you lift up while you're still here."

-Casey, in an earlier conversation, never forgotten

The breeze carried the scent of pine and wet soil—clean, unfiltered, familiar. From where Alex stood on the overlook deck at Northbend Collective, he could see the edge of the forest folding into the low hills beyond.

Wooden walkways meandered between glass meeting pavilions and open-air gathering spaces, offering a sense of peaceful seclusion. Teams met at stone fire pits. Laughter carried lightly over the sound of water running from a stream not far below. The whole campus felt like a breath of fresh air.

Alex sipped from the ceramic mug in his hand and heard the soft click of the door behind him.

"You weren't kidding," Casey said, stepping outside. "This place really does make Horizon Valley feel... industrial."

Alex turned, smiling as she crossed the deck. "I warned you," he said, nodding toward the view. "You trade elevator rides for sunrises out here."

Casey grinned, adjusting the cuffs of her jacket as she leaned against the railing beside him. "Sunrises and a full ecosystem of remote workers in fleece and trail shoes."

Alex laughed. "The Northbend aesthetic."

They stood silently for a few moments, letting the space speak first. That had become their rhythm—no forced updates or posturing, just presence. They had seen each other through enough transitions to trust the pauses.

"How's your team?" Alex asked.

Casey gave a proud nod. "Lisa's stepping into more than I even anticipated. Sharp, steady, asking the right questions. She doesn't fill the room. She shapes it."

Alex's chest warmed, something between pride and affirmation. "And Mark?"

"Just accepted a director role last week. Operations and Systems Integration. He brings calm without ever needing to raise his voice."

Alex let that settle, smiling softly. "I knew they'd rise."

"They had someone who believed in them first," Casey said, glancing sideways.

Alex exhaled slowly, then added, "It wasn't just about stepping aside. It was about stepping with them—until they found their own stride."

Casey nodded at that, the corner of her mouth lifting. "That's what legacy actually looks like."

The breeze shifted slightly. A few dry leaves danced along the deck boards. Casey turned toward him, sharper now.

"You've been sitting on something," she said.

Alex blinked. "What gives you that idea?"

"The mug tap," she said, nodding toward his hand. "You only do that when you're weighing a question."

He chuckled. "You really do remember everything."

"I remember the important things," Casey said.

He looked out again, the line of trees blurring slightly in the midday sun. Then, he said it. "I've been thinking about reaching out to Howard for a role here."

Casey didn't move. She didn't blink, just stayed still, grounded.

"As a consultant," Alex clarified. "Short-term. Strategic infrastructure audit. He knows systems. Knows how to spot blind spots I might be too close to see. But more than that, I want him to know he is valued, not just valuable. I think he needs a space that sees him differently."

Casey let a breath go through her nose, then nodded once. "So," she said slowly, "you've come full circle."

Alex nodded. "Maybe."

She turned toward him fully, her voice soft but steady. "Offering someone a second chance doesn't mean you've forgotten who they were. It means you've decided who you are."

He looked at her, the words settling deeper than expected.

"Leadership," she continued, "has less to do with power and more to do with perspective—especially when we're looking at people we once viewed in just one way."

He didn't answer right away. "I'm not trying to fix him," he said eventually. "And I'm not trying to save him, either."

"Good," she said. "Redemption doesn't come from us. We just leave the door unlocked. What they do with it is their choice."

Alex nodded. "Offering it just feels right."

"Then that's enough." Casey answered softly.

They stood again in the stillness, the forest humming beneath them. Somewhere below, wind chimes stirred faintly outside one of the collaborative studios.

"I was actually going to ask you something else," Casey added, turning her body toward his. "Collaboration."

He raised an eyebrow.

"Between Northbend Collective and Horizon Valley," she said. "Leadership development cohorts. Cross-learning. Quiet spaces for loud teams."

Alex's smile returned, broader this time. "I've got a few ideas already."

Casey tilted her head. "Of course, you do."

They walked back inside slowly. The conversation shifted to vision and structure, but the heart of it remained the same: two leaders who had shed their performance-driven approach and learned to lead with clarity, conviction, and care.

They didn't say it out loud, but both understood that this was more than a partnership between organizations. It was the outcome of trust that endured past the transition.

This connection became a living legacy: trust passed forward, remembered, and *multiplied.*

And it was just the beginning.

ABOUT THE AUTHOR

Ryan Crittenden, Ph.D., is a leadership coach, Army veteran, and founder of XL Coaching and Development. He holds a doctorate in Industrial and Organizational Psychology and is certified in Gallup CliftonStrengths, The Six Types of Working Genius, and the John Maxwell Team. Ryan equips leaders to grow by leading from who they are—not who they think they need to be.

Drawing from his military experience and years of coaching, Ryan blends strengths-based development with emotional intelligence to help leaders build trust, navigate uncertainty, and lead with purpose. His core belief: Leadership isn't about having all the answers—it's about asking better questions, fostering clarity, and empowering others to thrive.

Ryan's leadership philosophy is rooted in a formative experience early in his career. After being dismissed by one superior, another leader chose to connect with him on a personal level—a simple gesture that reshaped his view of leadership.

That moment fuels his conviction that leadership starts with connection.

In his work, Ryan challenges the myth that great leaders all look or act the same. Instead, he teaches that the most effective leaders lead authentically from their strengths, not through mimicry or perfectionism. Leadership, he believes, is measured by sustainable progress and meaningful impact.

Becoming the Compass is Ryan's debut leadership fable, written for emerging leaders navigating complexity, burnout, or a lack of guidance. Through storytelling and insight, the book offers practical lessons that can be applied individually or in teams—and revisited often.

The compass metaphor reflects Ryan's coaching style: helping leaders reconnect with their internal grounding so they can move forward with clarity and confidence. His work supports leadership development programs, workshops, and coaching across industries.

Outside of his professional life, Ryan is grounded by his faith, his wife, and his two sons. His approach is shaped not just by academic study, but by real-world experience—leading, failing, learning, and helping others rise.

Learn more at xlcoaching.net,

or connect with Ryan on LinkedIn
to continue the conversation.

Made in the USA
Columbia, SC
28 June 2025

60026364R00189